WORLDS AWAY:

FOLLOWING MY FATHER'S
WORLD WAR II FOOTSTEPS

Patrick M. Finelli

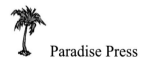

Paradise Press

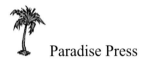
Paradise Press

Copyright © 2004 by Patrick M. Finelli, Ph.D.

Library of Congress Control Number: 2004094087
Finelli, Patrick M., 1949- -
Worlds Away: Following My Father's World War II Footsteps / Patrick M. Finelli
Includes bibliographic references.

ISBN 0-9754989-0-8
1. Finelli, Patrick M., 1949-   . 2. Peleliu Island, Battle of, 1944. 3. World War, 1939-1945 – Personal narratives-American. 4. United States Marine Corps – Biography. 5. Soldiers–United States–Biography.

Printed in the United States of America

Additional copies of this book are available through the web:

http://www.pfweb.com/pfdocs/contact1.htm

E-mail address: peleliu@pfweb.com

Cover photo: Author overlooking Bloody Nose Ridge and the invasion beaches from the observation deck on Peleliu.

Cover design: Leigh Bohne

Dedicated to my father and all of those who did their duty

Patrick L. Finelli, USMC in 1943

Table of Contents

Foreword

I met Dr. Pat Finelli in late 2004 when I took my son, Joe, to a lecture he gave at MacDill Air Force Base in Tampa, Florida regarding his research travels to the island of Peleliu for this book. The U.S. Navy had recently transferred me and my family back to the continental United States from the island of Guam in the Marianas chain, where I had served with a Naval Special Warfare (SEAL) unit.

My own father is a U.S. Navy veteran of World War II in the Pacific Theater, and I was particularly impressed by Dr. Finelli's lecture, because it centered around his own father who served as a U.S. Marine attached to Underwater Demolition Team SIX (UDT-6), and later as a Demolition Man attached to the 1st Marine Division at Peleliu in 1944. I myself was a Marine Infantry Officer for seven years in the 70s and 80s, before transferring to the Navy to become a SEAL, so I share the same dual heritage with the elder Mr. Finelli as a "Marine" and "Frogman." I'm looking forward to his next visit to Florida so my son and I can have lunch with him and his son. The UDT Frogmen of World War II are the forefathers of the modern day SEALs.

While stationed on Guam, I had the opportunity to travel to Peleliu with my son Joe in 2003. I was a former Marine, and stationed on Guam, just 800 miles north of Peleliu, a relatively short trip in the vast distances of the Pacific. I felt compelled to travel with my son to that sacred battleground about which I had heard and read so much during my 27 years of active military service. Joe was a newly certified scuba diver, so we decided to combine a dive trip to the Palau islands with a battlefield tour of Peleliu. Any diver reading this book will immediately identify with all the gadgets, terminology, scenery, excitement, and frustration mentioned listed in the detailed descriptions of the great diving in the picturesque paradise of Palau.

After a few days of diving the magnificent waters around the main island of Babeldaob, and viewing the superb World War II wrecks, fish, sharks, and clams, Joe and I boarded a small power boat for the ride to Peleliu. As we came ashore and stepped onto the island, I tried to see it as it had been in September of 1944. The blast furnace heat and drenching humidity were similar, but the foliage was not at all the same. Peleliu veteran and Medal of Honor recipient, Marine Major Everett Pope, provided a perfect quote for the title of chapter 7, "The Jungle Does Grow." Lush, green vegetation covered the island, in sharp contrast to the blasted and burned remains of the jungle that greeted the men of the 1st Marine Division.

Since we were tourists and not invaders, we wore only lightweight T-shirts, shorts, and sandals, versus the heavy "herringbone" utility uniforms, boots, ammo belts, packs, steel helmets, knives, entrenching tools, pistols, rifles, machine guns, mortars and other implements of war worn and carried by men during the fight for Peleliu. It is truly difficult to imagine how anyone survived Peleliu in combat. It was surely the grace of God that allowed any man to survive.

My son Joe and I also stayed at the Storyboard Resort on Peleliu. Our beach bungalow was already occupied by a spider with a leg span the size of my hand on the thatched ceiling, but the hotel proprietor assured me this arachnid would not be a nuisance to us. He wasn't.

Joe and I rented bikes from the hotel and set off to explore the battlefield by ourselves. Unfortunately, we did not have an expert guide like Tangie Hesus, but we made our way around the island just fine. Even though the entire island is a battlefield, we were initially drawn to invasion beaches White and Orange on the western coast. That is where the Marines hit the beach.

It was surprising to see how much combat debris and live ordnance remained on and near the beaches. Many metal caterpillar treads from Marine amphibious tractors (amtracs) lie on the beach and in the shallow water approaches. The large drive sprockets that drove these treads are also scattered about the area. Seeing these remnants made us acutely aware of the ferocity of the fight. Large, thick, heavy metal machine parts like these didn't just fall off armored vehicles. They had to be blasted off by high velocity, high explosive projectiles. Those same projectiles also tore through the Marines inside the vehicles.

Peleliu is still a dangerous place. The amount of live ordnance lying around in plain sight is astounding. Fifty-nine years of exposure to sun, rain, and salt water had, in many cases, only a mild effect on the brass casings of much of what we saw. Live mortar, anti-tank, machinegun and rifle ammunition was everywhere. We also found an American gas mask, bayonet handle, mess kit lid, and coffee cup, as well as Japanese barbed wire stakes, broken rice bowl fragments, and the ubiquitous Coca-Cola bottles from the 1940s.

On the beach, it was amazing to see a forty foot palm tree growing up through the remains of an abandoned amtrac. The treads, engine, and heavy side armor were mostly intact, but the deck had rusted through. It must have come to rest over a coconut in 1944, and that seed sprouted and spent the last 59 years growing through the remains of the destroyed vehicle. The jungle does indeed grow.

As we moved off the beach, we encountered numerous concrete pillboxes just inside the jungle. All had been attacked on that September morning in 1944, and they still bore the blast and burn scars of Marines who either conquered them or died trying. We viewed the large blockhouse which has been turned into a museum, but unfortunately it was closed, and we could only peer in through the dusty windows, and view the external holes breached in the building by the few fortunate naval gunfire impacts.

Our next stop was the airfield. Standing on the runway, it was easy to see how American attack pilots would take-off and 15 seconds later be doing their wheels-down bomb runs on Bloody Nose Ridge. The ridge was only spitting distance away from the airfield.

Riding to the base of Bloody Nose Ridge brought us to the 1st Marine Division Memorial, and also to the site of many Japanese memorials. After paying our respects at the Marine memorial, we hiked up to the peak of the hill where the 323rd Infantry Regiment memorial is located, and took in the scenery, as well as the words inscribed on the monument: "Lest we forget those who died." We only had to venture a few steps off the path to find hand grenade, mortar, and artillery shrapnel, as well as rifle and machinegun projectiles and shell casings. These artifacts bore mute testimony to the horrific battle sixty years ago.

While on the summit, we heard chanting drifting up from the jungle around and below us. We later learned that many Japanese people make trips to Peleliu to offer prayers for their ancestors and countrymen who were killed in the battle.

Our visit to Peleliu ended too soon. I am most grateful for the opportunity to visit the sacred ground on Peleliu with my son. We did it to learn about, and pay tribute to, those who went before us, and to those "Who foremost fighting fell" in the defense of our country. As a former Marine and currently serving SEAL, it meant a lot to me to share with Joe what I had read and heard about the battle, and it was important for him to actually walk the ground and see where the men fought and died for our great nation. We were both truly humbled by the experience. If I could change one thing about the trip, I would have done it in the company of the veterans who fought there.

World War II veterans are really something special. Even though they tell me how great "us guys" in uniform are today, I stand in awe of what they did when they were the ones wearing the cloth of our country. True, today's American fighting man has superb equipment and great training, but those World War II veterans had next to none of the technology nor training of those who serve today. They fought with their hearts and guts, and they saved the world.

As an active duty military man, I am compelled to remember our forefathers. Many of the old Marines and Frogmen of World War II are gone, but I am honored to be able to continue to uphold the very best traditions of the most elite warriors in the world while many of them are still alive to appreciate it. May God bless our memory of them.

David T. Pittelkow
Captain, U.S. Navy

Preface

My father's dress blue Marine uniform trimmed in red with its white frame cap left an indelible impression on me as a child. It had colorful rectangular battle ribbons, sharpshooter and weapons badges and other medals. I asked him about the Purple Heart and he told me it was for wounds he suffered while cleaning out caves on Peleliu.

Growing up in the 1950s, inevitably my friends and I asked each other, "What did your father do in the war?" Many of them had dads who fought in Europe and their first thought was always about D-Day. I'd say my father fought in the Pacific and they'd ask another question, "Iwo Jima, Guadalcanal or Okinawa?" I always responded with a place and battle that threw them for a loop: "Peleliu." No one had heard of it except for one well-read schoolmate who asked if I meant "Palau."

My father had his KA-BAR knife and several USMC combat training manuals. I would look through them for tips on jujitsu. I never told my friends that my father possessed a bloodstained Japanese flag.

Memory. Remembering. Reminiscences. What does it mean to remember? How is it possible to look at the past in the present? What is the essence of memory? How can we identify and separate historical memory from history itself? How can I formulate a mental image of something that happened in the past, specifically the memories formed by my own father's experience during World War II? How can he possibly transmit his memories to me?

One day in the summer of 2003, I interviewed my father. He talked about logistics and his deployments, but it became clear to me that it was exceedingly difficult for him to divulge the haunting memories of what actually took place in combat. Given the tremendous respect and admiration I have for my father, as well as for all the others who did their duty and fought on those battlefields worlds away, I knew I had to see Peleliu for myself. The next logical step was a determined decision to make my way to the place where military and personal history was forged in the crucible of fierce combat.

Although we may find maps, battle plans, artifacts, pictures, letters, and eyewitness accounts, they exist as fragments of an experience that historians encode as historical memory constructed long after the event itself has taken place. As a university professor, I initially wanted to take the historiographer's approach, setting aside considerations of objective reality and subjective response. As the son of a USMC combat veteran, I wanted to walk in my father's footsteps, to see what he saw, to try to imagine what he thought and felt, to blend his personal narrative with my own; sixty years afterward. A memory of the past does not arise out of merely "sensing" the evidence (by sight or touch), but of its essence (*eidos*) in our mind. There is an identity that is disclosed, deeper than the outward aspect that cannot be perceived with physical eyes, but becomes apparent in the mind's eye.

These concepts whirled in my mind as I began this journal on February 17, 2004. Nearly all of my writing during a 28-year academic career had been either technical or historiographic, examining complex systems and relationships, placing ideas and events in socio-cultural contexts, attempting to determine the essential characteristics that define historical evidence, and questioning the process of writing history.

When I applied for a faculty sabbatical after fourteen years since my last extended leave, it was an opportunity to redirect my focus toward something intensely personal. Perhaps it was convergence rather than divergence, as a vortex pulled my soul to the other side of the world.

The path to Peleliu began when my sister Chris suggested I turn my attention to telling my father's story. We quickly created a website as a tribute to my father, who kept a wartime journal when he served at Peleliu, Yap, and Ulithi in perilous combat. It is dedicated to the "greatest generation" out of respect for my father and others who fought the courageous Battle of Peleliu.

My sister encouraged the family to document our father's Marine Corps experience. My brother transcribed his personal war chronology. My mother has provided unwavering support, helping my father to negotiate the rugged shoals of painful recollection and distant memory.

My sister manages volunteers at a hospice. During her visits to see patients and check on their caregivers, she encounters many veterans and listens to stories about their wars—Vietnam, Korea, World War II and others. These men did their duty and use their last breaths to express what it meant to them. Many have led productive lives; others became lost in alcohol, depression and fear.

My father spent his entire post-war civilian career as a professional mechanical engineer, leading the development of major innovations and products. He holds many patents for his inventions, producing an outstanding legacy together with the best engineering minds of the 20th century. My father and mother were married in 1948, and are devoted to four adult children, who attained four undergraduate and six graduate degrees, and three talented granddaughters.

The links on our Peleliu tribute website listed at the end of this section include my father's wartime activities transcribed from his personal diaries, war journals, official records, documents and other pages on his site.

My father swam as a Marine substitute with the Navy's UDT-6 in the top-secret pre-invasion beach reconnaissance of Peleliu.[1] Later, he fought on the island with the 1st Pioneers shortly after the landing troops' assault, when the infantry met more resistance than they were led to expect.

He also saw duty on Yap, Ulithi, and many other islands in the Western Carolines in addition to the Marshalls and the Gilberts during two tours in the Far Western Pacific. He was hospitalized on Guam after being wounded by bayonet on Peleliu and in Hawaii at Naval Hospital #10, Aiea Heights, Pearl Harbor from October to December 1944 before returning to duty with his unit, MAG-45.[2]

He left the Pacific for the final time after another injury, a concussion at Yap, hospitalized at Ulithi, flown to Guam (Naval Hospital #103), then transported aboard a hospital ship to Oak

Knoll in Oakland, California and finally by hospital train across country to Chelsea Naval Hospital, Massachusetts.

I set the process in motion more than a year in advance as relentless forces drove me to embark upon a distant journey, far away in time, to the Pacific island battle zone that was a severe test for many young soldiers during World War II. Above all, I wanted to see the places that had made such a lasting and painful impression on my own father, a proud member of the 1st Marine Division during World War II who met his demons on the battlefields of Peleliu.

Less than two weeks away from departure in the spring of 2004, I was overcome with a combination of anticipation and apprehension. Eagerly looking forward to an incredible journey, I wasn't sure what to expect when I got there and explored the island that claimed so many lives during the Battle of Peleliu. My father said I'd hear voices. I was not going as a tourist. I wanted to find a connection to the memories of the past.

Will McFarland of World of Adventure in San Diego worked closely with me to customize an itinerary that would take me to Truk Lagoon (Chuuk) on the liveaboard dive boat *Truk Odyssey*. The actual planning process began in July 2003, when I found the *Truk Odyssey* was booked from January to June 2004 with the exception of one week, March 6-14. I took it despite having to share a room with someone I hadn't met previously.

It was important for me to see the somber remains of Operation Hailstone, where U.S. Navy aircraft carrier planes demolished the Japanese fleet at anchorage in February 1944. Although most military vessels had fled Truk Lagoon, the freighters and converted passenger ships along with a destroyer and a Betty Bomber provided more than a glimpse into the machines of war. The sunken ships with torpedo holes and bomb damage held a large amount of military hardware, ammunition, trucks, tanks, artillery shells, torpedoes, periscopes on the submarine tenders, and land-based artillery headed for the islands directly in the path of the Allied Forces led by General Douglas MacArthur and Admiral Chester Nimitz.

After Chuuk, my next stop would be in Yap followed by Palau and then Peleliu. Phil Orr, noted author, military archeologist and photojournalist who took the contemporary pictures for the Marine Monograph *Bloody Beaches*, generously provided detailed information about the location of important sites and the terrain on Peleliu. I felt as if I knew my way around the island already. Everett Pope, awarded the Medal of Honor for his gallantry in action during the Battle of Peleliu, graciously provided the contact information for Tangie Hesus, the best battlefield guide on Peleliu. Major Pope had traveled to the island for the 50th anniversary dedication of the Marine Memorial and Medal of Honor plaque across the Horseshoe Valley from the ridge he defended overnight in ferocious combat.

The Storyboard Resort on Peleliu was somewhat difficult to book, but my dates were flexible. After several e-mail exchanges between Mayumi, co-owner of the Storyboard Resort and Will McFarland, I managed to get a room for three days in late March. As it turned out, there were other accommodations on the island where I could have stayed in a pinch.

One good piece of advice my father gave me that applies to anyone planning such a trip is to get in shape. The travel is demanding, and it doesn't get easier once you are there. Swimming 2,500 meters every other day for almost a year and hiking a few miles on the off days helped considerably. Fortunately, our community pool in Temple Terrace, Florida is heated to 80 degrees year-round.

Although Florida's landscape is flat and doesn't approximate the steep limestone hills of Peleliu, walking is an excellent exercise for cardiovascular training. Combined with a slight change in my diet, I felt that I was physically ready for the rigors of scuba diving and trekking through the jungle.

My parents arrived a few days before I left to watch the house while I would be gone. I'd worked hard to get the property and myself in shape. I worried as much about them as they did about me. There were lots of details to take care of before leaving, but they all dissolved when I left Tampa International Airport.

This story's focus had to develop from my own journey to trace my father's footsteps in the Far Western Pacific during World War II. I had to observe, interpret, analyze and, more importantly, absorb its emotional impact.

Peleliu Tribute Website URL:

http://www.pfweb.com/plf-usmc/

Footnotes
[1] See chapter 7 for more details about the origin of the Underwater Demolition Teams (UDT), predecessors to the Navy SEALs.
[2] Marine Air Group (MAG).

chapter

Peleliu   1

Peleliu is a quiet, tropical island in the Western Carolines; a state in the Republic of Palau; a place where there are sandy beaches, limestone cliffs, caves, few road signs and many reminders of World War II. The war transformed this tranquil island into a fortress when Japanese forces, consisting of many veterans from the brutal campaign in Manchuria, displaced the Peleliuans and fortified the natural topography and geological features for the sole purpose of inflicting the greatest number of casualties on U.S. Marines. Peleliu became the scene of one of the bloodiest battles of World War II. Over 10,000 Japanese and 20,000 U.S. Marines were locked in mortal combat on a heavily fortified island of fifteen square miles with hard coral landing beaches, steep and treacherous limestone cliffs, and labyrinthine cave networks in blistering 115° F temperatures.

Late in his life, when an interviewer asked Bob Hope about his most moving experience while entertaining U.S. troops during a decades-long career, the comedian did not hesitate to solemnly reply that it was in Pavuvu, in a special show for the 1st Marine Division as they prepared to invade Peleliu. It had not been on his original itinerary. Pavuvu was itself a muddy, rat-infested Devil's Island. Later, Hope said that he believed 60% of those Marines died in the Battle of Peleliu.

The cost was high. The casualty rates were indeed about 60% for the Marine infantry regiments. The invasion began on September 15, 1944, and the 1st Marine Division suffered 4,000 casualties by September 22nd. Major Gordon D. Gayle was the Commanding Officer of the 2nd Battalion, 5th Marines. According to the official Marine monograph, *Bloody Beaches*, written by General Gordon D. Gayle, and published in observance of the 50th anniversary of victory in World War II, there were 6,526 Marine casualties with

1

1,252 killed when they left Peleliu as the Army arrived to close it out. The Army's 81st Division suffered 3,089 casualties with 404 killed in action. The Japanese defense strategy was based upon inflicting the greatest number of casualties and then to die. The result was over 10,000 Japanese casualties, and most of them were fatalities. Only 202 prisoners of war were taken and just 19 were Japanese military. The rest were Korean miners and workers.

The battle was supposed to be "quick but rough."[1] The command intelligence indicated that it would only take a few days. They were wrong. Eugene Sledge explains why: "The Japanese had constructed the perfect defense-in-depth with the whole island as a front line. They fought until the last position was knocked out. Aided by the incredibly rugged terrain, the new Japanese tactics proved so successful that the 1st Marine Division suffered more than twice as many casualties on Peleliu as the 2nd Marine Division had on Tarawa. Proportionately, United States casualties on Peleliu closely approximated those suffered later on Iwo Jima where the Japanese again employed an intricate defense-in-depth, conserved forces, and fought a battle of attrition."[2]

September 15, 1944 was D-Day on Peleliu, yet it wasn't until November 22 that Colonel Kunio Nakagawa, the commander of Japanese defense forces, sent his message to headquarters in Koror that the end was near. The code words to General Sadae Inoue were *Sakura, Sakura* and the final message went out on November 24. He wanted his wounded men to commit suicide and the rest to mount a final *banzai* charge. Nakagawa and General Kenjio Murai committed *seppuku*, ritual suicide, in a cave deep in the Umurbrogol pocket. Today, Nakagawa's telephone is mounted on a wall in the museum on Peleliu. Tangie Hesus, the pre-eminent Peleliu battlefield guide, let me pick it up and hold the receiver to my ear. It made my blood curdle.

The Umurbrogol Mountains bristled with labyrinthine cave systems reinforced with concrete, affording fortified protection from artillery and mortars for the entrenched enemy. The cave networks provided multiple openings with tunnels, entries and egresses for ambushes. The "mountains" are actually hills less

2

than 300 feet in elevation. The 1st Marines and the 7th Marines suffered severe casualties while attacking the craggy cliffs that contained Colonel Nakagawa's remaining forces. The fanatical enemy would fight to the death rather than surrender.

As the commander of the 2nd Battalion, 5th Marines on Peleliu, Major Gayle targeted the Umurbrogol for bombing runs on enemy positions. The Marine Corsairs took off from the captured airfield in short, wheels-down napalm drops. Today, the old Japanese airfield is Peleliu's airport. It only took about 10-15 seconds for Matt, our Australian pilot, to fly over the hills after take-off in his Belau Air Islander two-engine plane in 2004.

The Horseshoe Valley, where most of the Marines' heavy armor was deployed in the first weeks of October 1944, separates the East ridges, Walt's Ridge and Pope Hill, from the West. The resistance was fierce on the West ridges including Hill 300, Five Sisters, Five Brothers, China Wall, and the lower areas of Death Valley and Wildcat Bowl. Infantry attacks were the only way to penetrate the limestone cliffs.

Gailey describes the perilous situation: "It should be reiterated that safety was only relative on Peleliu anywhere in the vicinity of the highland regions. The Army's 321st RCT was still mopping up resistance in the north and taking casualties from the elusive Japanese who had been left behind.[3] The West Road, which had been considered secure since the 5th Marines' drive to the north, was still hazardous since Japanese snipers could slip onto the ridges overlooking the road and pick off unwary travelers. The most dangerous part of the road earned the dubious name of Dead Man's Curve."[4]

After visiting Peleliu in March 2004, a continuous stream of imagery stands out in my mind: scuba diving; betel nuts; battlefields; my guide, Tangie Hesus; storyboards; barracuda sashimi; schools of big-eyed jacks; trevally; and scores of sharks on every descent. Yet it all pales in comparison to the profound impression left by the invasion beaches, steep cliffs, treacherous caves and the debris of war on the island.

This story cannot be measured by depth or pressure gauges. The

Peleliu battlefield is on the other side of the world, and our eyes were focused elsewhere on different wars in 2004. Yet, although Peleliu is far away in time and place, it provided a defining moment in the history of the 1st Marine Division and the young Marines who went into battle. One of them was my father.

Why take Peleliu? General Douglas MacArthur was moving on the west toward the Philippines and Fleet Admiral Chester Nimitz took the eastern route. Admiral William Halsey had doubts about the need to take Peleliu, but MacArthur convinced him that he needed the airfield to protect his left flank. The Marines of the 1st Division were told it would be a rough, three-day walkover. The battle raged for months. The beach was more than 200 yards from the fringing reef at its closest point. The landing beaches were covered with heavily fortified enfilading fire. The hard coral on the White Beaches extends all the way to the jungle where the enemy was entrenched despite the pounding of U.S. Navy battleships for several days.

Much of the official literature and many personal narrative accounts describe the battle as a "meat grinder." Eight Marines were awarded the Medal of Honor for conspicuous gallantry in action, including Captain Everett P. Pope, Commander of "C" Company, 1st Battalion, 1st Marines, who graciously helped me learn what to do and what to expect on Peleliu. Pope was promoted to the rank of Major before he put down his sword at the end of the war.

Major Gayle was awarded the Navy Cross for his heroism on Peleliu, and retired as a Brigadier General after an exceptional 30-year career in the Marines. General Gayle provided extraordinary insight about the Battle of Peleliu

> My most difficult conclusion respecting the Peleliu campaign has had to do with whether or not the entire undertaking may have been unnecessary. Having lost 50% of my men, and 60% of my officers in the campaign, this is a most difficult conclusion to embrace. The best I have been able to do is to entertain the thought that it _may_ not have been necessary. The fog of war certainly enveloped that strategic choice. We now know that the February strike against the Palaus more effectively neutralized that strong point than we realized. But

that sets us toward questioning the need for the larger undertaking of "returning" to the Philippines. My conclusion is that it was an emotional and ego driven campaign, not particularly a logical one.[5]

When you ask most veterans to tell their story, many can remember places, dates, weapons and the inevitable stench of war. Few feel comfortable telling what it was really like for them. Everett Pope told me that many who served and survived the Battle of Peleliu suffered from nightmares and trauma, even while raising families and establishing civilian careers. I believe this is true for many who have been in combat. A common retort is, "You had to be there to truly understand."

Everett Pope gave me Tangie's name and number, and Tangie had replied with a confirming e-mail to me in December 2003. Tangie was an extraordinarily valuable companion and friend. He has the utmost respect for Major Pope and carried a copy of Pope's Medal of Honor Citation Folio when we climbed Pope Hill. I believe he also gave me special attention because of my father and all the other Marines and soldiers who fought on his island. When I met other Peleliuans, they smiled and greeted me with a warm welcome. Many of the elders had been displaced prior to the Japanese occupation, and the United States Armed Forces gave them their island back after improving the roads, airfield and infrastructure with electricity and water.

My family set up a tribute website for my father's World War II experience long before I began this book. The response from others, unsolicited and extremely personal, was overwhelming. Sons, daughters, nephews and nieces of Peleliu veterans sent touching notes and recollections about their fathers and uncles. The outpouring of sentiment from those with loved ones, living and dead, who fought on Peleliu has touched me deeply.

Rob Amaral told me about his uncle Ed from Bridgewater, Massachusetts, who was one of the first to cross the airfield. Here is an excerpt from his citation:

"Sergeant Edward Amaral received the Bronze Star Presidential Citation for heroic achievement while serving as Squad Leader, Marine Assault Rifle Company B, 1st Battalion, 5th Marines, 1st

Marine Division, in action against enemy Japanese forces on Peleliu, Palau Islands from 15 to 25 September 1944. On one occasion, when his men attempted to take cover from hostile mortar fire under a cliff after their craft had struck rocks during landing, he stood up in an exposed position and led his men forward over a steep ledge to the side of an airstrip and, walking upright 250 yards through the intense mortar and machine gun barrage, hunted hostile pillboxes and installations."

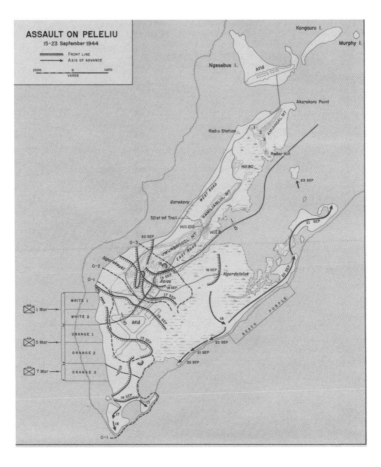

Peleliu Battle Plan, 15-23 September 1944.
(Courtesy Center of Military History, U.S. Army)

Footnotes

[1] James Hallas, *The Devil's Anvil: The Assault on Peleliu*, Westport, Connecticut: Praeger Publishers, 1994, p. 255.

[2] Eugene Sledge, *With the Old Breed: At Peleliu and Okinawa*, Novato California: Presidio Press, 1981, p. 53.

[3] Regimental Combat Team (RCT).

[4] Harry A. Gailey, *Peleliu 1944*, Annapolis, Maryland: The Nautical & Aviation Publishing Company of America, 1983, pp. 163-164.

[5] General Gordon D. Gayle, letter to author, 6 August 2004.

chapter

Getting There 2

The Continental flight was late leaving Tampa.   It was smart of Will at World of Adventure to book me to Houston overnight.   Otherwise, I risked missing the morning flight to Guam. Security at the airport was tight and the eight "C" cell batteries in my dive light caused some concern at the TSA checkpoint until I showed them the instruction manual. The HID ionized gas lamp was too fragile to pack in checked baggage, so I carried it in my backpack. After the recent train bombing tragedy in Madrid, backpacks came under careful scrutiny.

My parents had arrived safely from Boston before I left. We had a few days together. Dad would swim in the heated outdoor community pool and they'd both read several books and go to Mass every morning. After all, it was Lent. I took them up to the pool because the one in the backyard was still too cold and Dad and I swam an hour in adjacent lanes.

Dad gave me his aluminum dog tag for good luck.   It had his name, serial number, the letters USMC, his blood type, the date of his last tetanus shot, and his religion. I would wear it on a chain around my neck until I found Hill 260 on Peleliu.

After a quiet night in Houston, I rose early at 6:30 A.M., shaved, showered, re-packed and waited for the one-mile transfer to Houston International Airport. My next stop would be Hawaii. Guam passengers make a change of planes in Honolulu (with the same flight number—CO 001). I was excited about a week of diving aboard the *Truk Odyssey* in Chuuk Lagoon, recommended by many as the best liveaboard diving yacht in the world. It was hard to imagine what I would see while exploring the World War II shipwrecks at the bottom of the lagoon.

The flight from Houston to Hawaii was uneventful. I always fly with noise-canceling headsets, plenty of water and a filtration mask. Since the flight was almost eight hours, I walked up and down the aisles to avert Deep Vein Thrombosis (DVT). According

9

to some reports, sitting motionless for a long time may increase the risk of blood clotting in your legs, sometimes called "Economy Class Syndrome," where there is not much room. There are a few exercises I could do in my seat, but I wanted to move around every hour or so just to keep the blood flowing in my lower extremities. Coincidentally, during one of my jaunts about the cabin, I struck up a conversation with a fellow passenger and scuba diver named Paul Rogers. He was a former Navy flyer and pilot for a major airline. It turned out he was headed to the *Truk Odyssey*. His sister was flying from Los Angeles to meet him in Hawaii for the flight to Guam and the scuba diving adventure ahead.

Waiting at the gate for the Guam flight in Honolulu, there were many veterans wearing caps with the logo, "Military Historical Tours." I sat down next to one fellow who introduced himself as Red from Pennsylvania. He fought with the 4th Marine Division on Iwo Jima. His son accompanied him. I showed Red my father's dog tags and he displayed his own.

I mentioned Doctor John Wick, known as "Chichi Doc" for his service on Chichi Jima. Doc, a Pennsylvania ophthalmologist, had contacted me more than a year earlier through my father's tribute website. He had forwarded information about the Chichi Marine reunion. Red knew Doc Wick very well and had been to his office recently.

Doc Wick sent the defense plan for Iwo Jima to Dad along with other materials after my father distributed printed copies of the original defense plan for Chichi Jima at the Chichi Marine reunion. The defense plan for Chichi was crafted by Major Yoshitaka Horie, Japanese officer in charge at Chichi Jima, the central base of supply and communication between Japan and the Bonin Islands. Major Horie wrote it on December 23, 1945. He was the "star witness"[1] in the war crimes trials against the Japanese officers condemned to death for committing atrocities against eight pilots who had crash landed during bombing raids on Chichi Jima. Horie's defense plan fell into the hands of my uncle, a Navy radarman on LST 871, and is reprinted in appendix E of this book.

As my sister is fond of saying, "There are no coincidences." Meeting the veterans headed for Tinian, Saipan, and a memorial service on Iwo Jima was a reminder of the reason for my trip. The captain of our flight announced the presence of the veterans on board and their destination as we approached Eniwetok. The passengers erupted in applause. The Discovery Channel was along to film their journey. We arrived in Guam after crossing the International Date Line, and I had a brief layover before flying to Truk. The other passengers scattered to the gates for their final destinations in Micronesia upon landing in Guam.

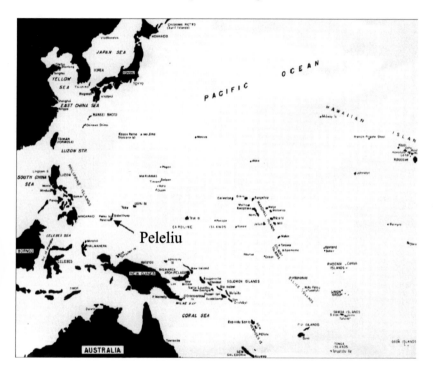

Peleliu Location (Courtesy of Marine Historical Division)

Footnotes
[1] James Bradley, *Flyboys*, Boston: Little, Brown and Company, 2003, p. 318.

3

Full Moon Over Truk Lagoon

Truk Lagoon contains many atolls and a surrounding reef. It was an ideal anchorage for the Japanese fleet with an airport, seaplane base, submarine base, main and repair anchorage; at least until the U.S. Navy's lethal attack known as Operation Hailstone in February 1944.

We arrived at the airport in Truk (Chuuk) after a brief layover in Guam, a modern airport, but not nearly as plush or extensive as the major airports in the United States. The next stop for the flight after landing in Chuuk was Pohnpei, followed by termination in Kosrae. The airport in Chuuk is not much more than a concrete building, open to the air, with the baggage claim to the right and immigration and customs on the left, less than 50 feet apart as you enter from the arrival gate. No frills here.

My bags were the first ones to appear. After clearing immigration and customs, Lenny, the captain of the *Truk Odyssey*, and his crew loaded our luggage into a van while directing the divers into their bus for the ride to the dock where a tender took us out to the ship. My initial impression of Truk during the drive from the airport to the dock at the Blue Lagoon Resort was one of abject poverty. Although it was dark, the road was unmistakably narrow, gutted with potholes. We saw a pickup truck with eight young policemen stop a driver on the other side of the road.

As I looked out the window of the bus with our sixteen divers and a Japanese driver, all I could see were dilapidated shacks and broken-down concrete structures. Fences and iron bars protected the blighted properties. I saw one window air conditioner unit that had bars around it. There were two small stores and a gas station.

The slum-like conditions rivaled Jamaica, Haiti and parts of any major U.S. city. I was glad to be sleeping on the boat tonight.

It looked better in daylight, however, when I saw the same stretch on the return trip. At that time, I realized there were two banks, a post office, the Truk Stop Motel, a playing field, fuel storage tanks, a port with shipping containers, a fishing fleet, and stores along the route.

As we entered the gate at the Blue Lagoon, the grounds were well lighted and manicured with royal palms and extensive landscaping. No wonder. The resort was formerly a Japanese seaplane base and then a coconut plantation before the Continental Hotel purchased it as a destination resort property. The legendary Chuuk diver Kimiuo Aisek bought it from the hotel chain. It has changed hands again since Aisek passed away.

As soon as our bags arrived onboard, we set up our dive gear. After a basic orientation, we prepared for a good night's sleep before the next day's dives on the *Yamagiri Maru* (Misty Mountain) and the *Shinkoku Maru* (Divine Country), both not far from the main atoll of Moen. Our morning dive briefing would be at 7:30 A.M. the next day. I could hardly sleep.

Cabin #9 on the *Truk Odyssey* was a double with two bunk beds. A rescue diver from Fairfield, Massachusetts named Jim slept in the bunk above. Jimbo and his four dive buddies (Moe, Don, and two fellows named Steve) had arrived from Palau. I asked them about diving the Rock Island reefs, in particular Blue Corner. Many technical divers prefer caves and wrecks to reef diving, and Jimbo was no exception. Although impressed with the diving in the Republic of Palau, he was in another zone among the wrecks of Truk Lagoon. Jimbo and Steve (the one who worked for Raytheon) went over the bow on our deepest dive later in the week. The caption on the DVD recording of the dive said, "202' Baby."

I rose before dawn and was on deck at 5:00 A.M. with plenty of time for writing in my journal. Early risers the first morning had an opportunity to snap photographs of the full moon while waiting for sunrise, the rest of the passengers, and the crew. Konta was on the diving deck. He stays up all night and sleeps during the day, performing a crucial watchman role for the ship.

Our first dive was to the *Yamagiri Maru*, a 439' passenger ship

14

converted into a cargo carrier. It rested on its port side in 110 feet of seawater in the shipping lane southwest of the main island Moen (Weno) and northwest of Fefan Island.

Full moon aft of the *Truk Odyssey* (Photo © 2004 Patrick Finelli)

We found a large torpedo hole in the keel just forward of the superstructure, a nice spot to penetrate the wreck and swim through its steel beams. As we expected after sixty years, there was a lot of marine growth under the bow and stern, and it had dense soft coral on the propeller. The stern hold contained 18-inch artillery shells, the largest available at the time, to supply the battleships *Musashi* and *Yamamoto*.

There was a "Y" insignia on the smokestack representing Yamashita, the owners of the ship. An interesting feature was the ship's telegraph on the stern to communicate speed changes between the deck and the engine room. There was a bow gun in the sand. It was a relatively easy dive since the depth averaged around 75 to 85 feet.

Truk Lagoon[1] (Copyright © 2000 Dan E. Bailey. Reprinted with permission.)

Most of the group consisted of advanced technical, cavern and rescue divers; many used double tanks, H-valves, redundant first stages. Nearly everyone used Nitrox. One diver had a custom-made rebreather. I decided to take a 112 cubic inch steel tank with compressed air. It took a couple of dives to establish proper weight for neutral buoyancy and I settled on 4 lbs. integrated into my Scubapro® "Glide Plus" buoyancy jacket.

The next dive was at the *Shinkoku Maru*, a 10,000-ton, 500'-long naval transfer ship. It lies upright on a slope with the stern at a depth of 130', the bow at 105', and a torpedo hole at 125' on the port side near the smokestack. There were two masts and a king post with an abundance of marine growth; columns of coral, nudibranchs, batfish, snapper, many sea anemones, bright orange clownfish (*Amphiprion ocellaris*) with their distinctive three white bands edged in black and many of "Nemo's" anemone fish friends, and delicately moving lionfish (*Pterois volitans*). There

16

was a ship's telegraph on the stern for communicating speed to the engine room. A few divers spotted a manta ray off the bow, a rarity in Chuuk Lagoon.

The bridge and other levels on the *Shinkoku* contained many of the crews' personal effects: shoes, mess kits, teakettles, china, bottles, gas masks, an operating table, tubs and toilets; eerie reminders that we were not diving ships sunk intentionally as dive sites, but places where men lived and died. Although the *Shinkoku* was a tanker ship, there were large deck guns mounted fore and aft.

I learned a few words of Chuukese from the back of the menu in the *Odyssey's* restaurant:

Hello	Ran annim
Good morning	Nesor annim
How are you?	Ifa usum
Fine	Pechekkun
Thank you very much	Kinisou chapur
Thank you	Kinisou
Thanks	So
You're welcome	Kete puan afani
I'm hungry	Ua echik
Delicious meal	Fakkun anno
Out of sight!	Anaparrap
I've finished	A wes

Jimbo had a little problem with the porthole on the top bunk n our room. He discovered water from a leak had soaked his bedding. There was nothing anyone could do right away except for him to move to one side of the bed. At least the bottom bunk was all right. I was usually up at 5:00 A.M. each morning; shaving with my miner's lamp in the mirror trying not to disturb Jim. I had done three dives the first day; the Nitrox divers did two more. Diving with compressed air stretches the no-decompression limits, even with a dive computer. It is extremely important to monitor built-up nitrogen in the blood and make safety stops according to the requirements of individual dive profiles to gas-off the residual nitrogen during repetitive dives. I took a conservative path.

Truk was called the "Pacific Gibraltar." It is a beautiful spot with wide anchorages. You can see from the photograph below that the atolls surrounding the lagoon offer high ground for observation and defense. The loss of forty ships in two days was a major defeat for the Japanese forces and a victory for the U.S. Navy. These islands were the last things the Japanese sailors saw before their ships sank.

Moen atoll in Truk Lagoon. (Photo © 2004 Patrick Finelli)

Wreck diving is both challenging and intriguing. It is an eerie swim through broken steel and sharp metal, often near personal artifacts like delicate bowls, cups, and fragile bottles completely intact. There is spectacular marine life with soft corals and anemones surrounded by clouds of baitfish, butterfly fish, wrasse, jacks and fairy basslets, particularly clustered around the large king posts and masts where many species have established their habitat. After penetrating the wreck, divers see weapons of war. This watery grave of the Pacific is now a paradise for advanced divers. My deepest dive during the trip was the *San Francisco Maru* at 170 feet—a technical decompression dive beyond the

18

limits of most sport diving.

Although my final objective of Peleliu was still weeks away, I learned quite a lot about what to expect while scuba diving in Chuuk on the *Truk Odyssey*. Truk Lagoon (as it is known to most Westerners) reveals a great deal about some of the important strategies and outcomes in the Pacific during WWII. It gave me an extraordinary respect for the Navy, and the dangers faced by the Marines.

The success of Operation Hailstone against the Japanese naval base in Truk Lagoon in February 1944 was an important factor in the Pacific war. Admiral Nimitz had moved his ships to the Marianas, bypassing the Carolines and the Japanese base at Chuuk. Admiral Spruance, Deputy Commander-in-Chief for the Pacific Fleet and Pacific Ocean Areas, made the decision to harass the island with nine carriers, six battleships, 10 cruisers and 28 destroyers. Hellcats, Avengers and Dauntless dive-bombers from the carriers *Enterprise*, *Essex*, *Belleau Wood*, *Intrepid*, *Bunker Hill* and the second *Yorktown* (the first was lost at Midway) conducted an effective raid. It was far more lethal than the Japanese attack on Pearl Harbor.

Japanese Vice Admiral Takeo Kurita's 2nd Fleet left Truk after seeing and hearing too many reconnaissance aircraft. Two USMC PB4Y Liberators from the grass airstrip on Stirling Island in the Western Solomons photographed the anchorage on February 5, 1944. Kurita must have known something was going to happen; he fled to Palau, 1,175 miles away, with many battleships and destroyers. Truk is 1,800 miles from Tokyo, but the merchant ships and freighters of the 4th Fleet were left behind and went to the bottom after the U.S. Navy attack, where they remain for scuba divers and nautical archeologists to explore. We discovered they were filled with extensive supplies of ammunition, heavy artillery and shells, detonators, torpedoes, tanks, planes with spare propellers and wings, hemispherical beach-type mines, trucks, bulldozers, mortar rounds, cordite, and the ubiquitous sake bottles.

Although many of my fellow scuba divers were fascinated and ecstatic over exploring the many wrecks in Truk Lagoon including one destroyer, a submarine, and a Betty Bomber, my enthusiasm was tempered with the realization of the additional deadly weaponry our forces might have faced as they moved north through the islands toward Japan. Were it not for the U.S. Navy's air attack, these weapons would have made it to the killing fields of the Pacific. I saw the same type of tanks, bullets and mortar rounds at the bottom of Truk Lagoon as I would later see in the caves, on the beaches, scattered over the ridges, and near the airfield on Peleliu.

Peleliu, Saipan, Iwo Jima, and Okinawa were tough battles in WWII, but if the ordnance and supplies had made it through, it may have been even more detrimental to the allies' success in battle. I have to salute the Navy for what they accomplished at Truk Lagoon.

The effectiveness of the air strike was unequivocal as each wreck had huge torpedo holes, bombed-out holds, or entire stern sections crumpled into debris. More than one looked like it took a bomb through its funnel (smokestack). It must have been a ferocious attack, with much more force than was used against the United States at Pearl Harbor. The juxtaposition of ceramic bowls, mess kits and intact bottles in close proximity to deformed steel beams and twisted metal was enigmatic; like the Titanic, only with machines of war.

One freighter, the *Fujikawa*, has a plaque in tribute to Kimiuo Aisek. He was an eyewitness to Operation Hailstone as a teenager, and remembered where the ships went down relative to the atolls. He was instrumental in pinpointing locations before sonar and thus began the Truk Lagoon diving industry. Aisek's contribution is well documented in Dan E. Bailey's *World War II Wrecks of the Truk Lagoon*. Bailey also lists the results of the first side-scan sonar expedition by Jacques Cousteau in the 1960s that found most of the remaining wrecks, which have become an important part of the Truk diving experience.

It was unlike any diving I had ever done since most sunken ships in my part of the world were intended to be artificial reefs and dive sites, or are much older like the Spanish galleons and British East India transports. For the most part it was a somber and moving experience. Though my enjoyment was tempered with the knowledge of events and battles of WWII, it was an experience I will never forget.

There were many interesting personalities among my fellow divers. A Canadian/Russian couple from Toronto proved to be expert underwater photographers. Two fellows from West Virginia were aboard. One of them, Kevin, had an elaborate re-breather rig. It was designed for cavern diving by a specialist in Florida. He did not leave any air bubbles in his wake and seemingly could stay down forever as his gas mixture adjusted constantly with time and depth. Other divers were retired military, active emergency rescue divers working with police and fire departments, and highly trained technical divers. One remarked that he was used to visibility of less than four feet, as he salvaged cars that people accidentally drive off bridges into rivers. The visibility in Truk Lagoon regularly exceeded 100 feet.

The food on the Truk Odyssey was excellent from breakfast through dinner. We enjoyed many freshly made snacks during the day. One afternoon we were treated with oatmeal cookies right out of the oven; another day we ate tender melt-in-your-mouth sashimi. Breakfast of the day was cooked to order: omelets, French toast or standard American fare. Dinners were up to the standards of the best restaurants in Micronesia. Asian cuisine, lobster tails, steak, and tuna were featured menu items. There were always unlimited beverages like iced tea, soft drinks and Kool-Aid® to help quench the divers' thirst.

The second day's dives included three ships: *Fumitzuki*, *Hanakawa Maru* and *Sankisan Maru*. The *Fumitzuki* is a 320′ Mutsuki Class Destroyer, just to the west of Moen. Its name means "the 7th month of the moon calendar when rice flowers."[2] Since it was a warship, it does not have the suffix *Maru*, which designated freighters, passenger vessels and cargo ships. Most wrecks were at anchor facing in the direction of the trade winds that blow out of the northeast, but the *Fumitzuki* faced south on the sandy bottom listing toward port suggesting she drifted before sinking.

The wreck had a few lionfish and the usual pipe rail coral and fish habitats. The debris included a lot of war material: torpedo tubes and controls for launching them, floats for setting the minesweeping paravanes at the right depth; bronze artillery shell casings; depth charge launchers; a 4.7-inch gun with ammunition; a propeller in the sand; pans; bottles, and personal artifacts.

The *Hanakawa Maru* was a 367′ tanker carrying barrels of aviation fuel. Consequently, the cargo holds are off-limits because of aviation fuel leaks. The ship suffered severe damage, and flaming fuel started fires on shore during the attack. I could almost smell the gases and lime as we anchored over the site. Avgas is quite toxic and can burn your skin if you are not careful. I thought that the ship should be called "Poison River," the opposite of the actual translation of its name, "Flower River."

The hull lay upright toward the west of the lagoon near Tol Island. It took over an hour for the *Odyssey* to get there from the *Fumitzuki*. After splashing into the water and descending, I noticed a large hole at the location of the funnel (smokestack) and a devastating torpedo hole on the starboard side between holds #1 and #2.

The *Hanakawa* hosts a proliferation of marine growth on the anchor chain, king post and masts: anemones, sea fans and lionfish. I saw the stern gun; a truck on the deck; and lots of china and bowls, bottles and washbasins. My dive light, an Underwater Kinetics® Light Cannon 100 HID, worked superbly, lighting up everything with a clear, bright beam. I peeked into windows and doors that lacked easy swim access.

Harty, the divemaster, and I set up a display with china, hand-painted cups and bowls. Although the ship sank in under 5 minutes fragile bottles and chinaware survived. Cara, co-owner of the *Odyssey* with her husband Lenny, said the wreck is not one where you should anchor overnight, perhaps because of the aviation fuel or the proximity to Tol Island.

The *Sankisan Maru* was a 380′ cargo ship, as evidenced by the booms and heavy equipment on the deck. The vessel rests on the bottom toward the west of Uman Island. It was the first time took a GPS reading of a location in Micronesia (N 07° 24.911′, 151° 44.388′).

This shipwreck contained three Isuzu trucks; their rusted skeletal remains were recognizable. One truck's steering wheel was still in place along with its four tires, but seawater and time had eroded the chassis and frame. Two trucks were on the port side and one was on the starboard. It was unbelievable to see tires over 60 years old looking like you could ride on them today. They must have been new when the ship went down, since there was plenty of tread. I checked for the brand, but could not read the label. Steel bends and breaks, but tires last a long time underwater.

Among the other debris were thousands of bullets, ammunition belts, containers and holds filled with aircraft engines, truck frames and tires. The wreck was broken and shattered at the stern, but it was at a relatively shallow depth since the keel lay at 100 feet. About half the ship remained.

Shortly after we arrived at the wreck, another contingent of divers from a different boat splashed into the water and spoiled the visibility with silt. When I returned to the bow, the holds were cloudy with oozing particles. Fortunately, it had been pristine when I went through the first time. My dive light illuminated the main artifacts and I had seen just about everything before they spoiled the visibility.

This was virtually a night dive. We began at dusk and darkness fell while we were exploring the wreck. Among the other discoveries were an airplane engine fuselage, a puffer fish, and more bottles.

One of the fellows from West Virginia had some trouble with a seal on this dive. He developed a leak in the housing and destroyed his new Canon® Power Shot S-40 digital camera. We watched with a mixture of sympathy and amazement as he took the camera apart in the ship's salon after dinner. Someone said he should just upgrade to the S-50, but he already had it in pieces on the dining table. After he put it back together, there were four screws left over.

I sat with a couple from Chicago in their second week on the *Odyssey*. I asked them about Friday's dive, to the *San Francisco Maru*. I was concerned since the deck was at a depth of 165' and would be flying the following day for Guam and Yap. They told me everyone dives with compressed air. We would go in groups of five with planned decompression stops. I was looking forward to it. I would trust my dive computer to indicate the decompression stops and when it would be safe to fly.

Divers would disappear from time to time during the cruise. It was safe to assume they were downloading their dive computer information into a personal computer where they could analyze their residual nitrogen and dive profile.

Dessert that night was a blueberry crepe after a main course of roasted chicken, scalloped potatoes and salad. Normally I would expect to gain weight with a menu like this, but I hoped the constant diving would keep it down.

The next day's dives were on the *Hoki Maru* and then the rest of the time we planned to spend on one of the most noteworthy wrecks: the *Fujikawa Maru*. The *Hoki Maru* was a deep wreck that lay upright on the lagoon floor. It is 450′ long and in good condition, at least the parts of the ship that remained. There was a huge gap between the bow and the stern due to serious bomb damage. It was completely demolished from an explosion, probably a secondary detonation of aviation fuel suggested by the off-limits first hold with leaking barrels of aviation gasoline. Many of the reconnaissance photographs taken during Operation Hailstone showed this ship exploding since it was first in the anchorage of the 4th Fleet.

I could see the charred metal, yet right above it there was a china bowl with a flag logo and several sake bottles, cups and glass housings for lighting fixtures. The hold on the aft side of the mast contained bulldozers, trucks, a tractor and steamroller. One large bulldozer was precariously balanced on a bent steel I-beam with truck frames underneath. We did not want to dive under the bulldozer, but we dove around it to explore the trucks at a depth of 135 feet.

I decided upon a conservative dive profile at this point with 35 minutes of bottom time because my dive computer had not cycled off since the first dive at the beginning of the week. The dive computer recorded my maximum depth and bottom time in its dive mode. It indicated the need for decompression during the dive. Afterward, it counted the surface interval. A blinking symbol of an airplane continued until it was safe to fly. Then the computer shuts itself off. Since it hadn't cycled off yet, it was important to make a slow ascent and take two decompression or safety stops.

I took a GPS reading as we motored between *Hoki* and *Fujikawa* (N 07° 20.885', E 151° 53.683') and then again at the *Fujikawa* (N 07° 20.678', E 151° 53.102').

The *Fujikawa Maru* is one of the most superb wreck dives in the world. The *Truk Odyssey* staff gave us plenty of time over this wreck and suggested four dives to explore it. It was an extraordinary wreck for experienced divers, truly one of the best imaginable. Originally built as a 437-foot passenger vessel with large cargo compartments, the ship was used as an aircraft ferry. It rests just south of the former Japanese airfield at Eten Island. The American bombers attacked the airfield first to knock out the enemy's planes, and then turned their attention to the ships. The *Fujikawa Maru* was at anchor when hit. The *Odyssey* tied off at its anchor chain.

The ship's holds contain Japanese Zero fighter planes complete with controls, seats, and large spare parts like propellers and wings. I started by exploring the three or four Zero fighter planes below deck, then went to the heavily encrusted bow gun with boxes of ammunition and a small, hard-to-find plaque that had an inscription indicating it is a 6-inch breech-loader with serial number 12469, manufactured by a British company (Elswick Ordnance) doing business with the Japanese Imperial Navy. It was made in 1899, according to the date on the plaque.

Shortly afterward, I met up with Harty on the wreck. He was one of the best divemasters in the lagoon, and I followed him back down into the labyrinth below. The engine room contained identifiable components such as handles and mechanical indicators for the ship's speed control. The steering compartment had a bronze covered compass mounted on its binnacle.

There was so much to see on this wreck, it was not surprising we dived on it more than the rest of the ships. The sights included electrical insulators, machine guns, more than one ship's telegraph, depth-charge containers, cylinders, hoses, barrels, china, mess kits, numerous ammunition shells, crates of sake bottles and a rice cooker. There were cavernous companionways with soft corals and narrow corridors with metal grids, ship's ladders and tight swim-throughs. Long vistas were broken only by stalactite-like corals covering broken metal with encrusted wiring draped along the halls in the superstructure. It was eerie, fascinating and challenging.

Additionally, there is a metalworking shop that looked like you could start an underwater vocational training center complete with clamps, vises, lathe, drill press and shelves with springs and spare parts. We swam through the tool room and saw an air compressor nicknamed R2D2. It really did look like a robot staring out through a window as we swam down a companionway to the entrance down the stairs.

Although it was a complex and interesting wreck to penetrate, it wasn't an exceptionally deep dive. We could see everything within a depth of 105 feet.

We had to make sure we had proper buoyancy, since some of the passages were skinny, and we had to avoid kicking up silt. We swam down and out through the torpedo hole, about 105', then back up to explore the kitchen, baths, sake distillery, and hundreds of intact sake bottles along with shattered remnants. The plentiful shards of glass appeared dangerous, but they were not threatening to us as we floated in perfect weightlessness. We swam through more narrow passages, corners and turns. The HID dive light bathed the artifacts with brilliant illumination.

We ended our initial dive on this astonishing shipwreck at two plaques next to each other on the deck forward of the superstructure (control room) and aft of the bow gun. One commemorates the lethal attack; the other praises Kimiuo Aisek as "The Greatest Diver in the Pacific." Harty paused at the one for Aisek, and rubbed it clean with his gloves.

I thanked Harty after the dive. He told me Kimiuo was his grandfather and another divemaster on the boat is his uncle. It was a moving experience. With Harty's expert guidance, I saw more than most divers. I decided to go back again later for a twilight or night dive.

Most of the divers used Nitrox and completed four or five dives a day. However, using compressed air with the depth and frequency in these dives required careful attention to safety stops. I vowed to get certified for Nitrox in Yap, the next stop on my journey. For now, I tried to be very conservative in my dive profiles. The next day we were headed for the reef to feed the sharks. Friday would be the deep technical dive on the *San Francisco Maru*, when everyone would be on compressed air at a 21% oxygen level.

The history of western civilization is replete with references to explorers "discovering" other lands. Polynesians migrated to the islands of Hawaii 1,500 years before English Captain James Cook "discovered" the islands in 1778. Carib, Arawak and Taino cultures existed long before Columbus "discovered" the New World in 1492. The first circumnavigator of the world, Portuguese explorer Ferdinand Magellan, "discovered" and died in the Philippines in 1521. In the same way, when the Spanish explorer Alonso de Arellano "discovered" Kwajalein and Chuuk in 1565, the Chuukese people were already living there. The German Protectorate began in 1885, and they sold the islands to the Japanese during World War I. The 1916 Japanese census counted 13,300 Chuukese.

Prior to arrival, I had read about Xavier High School in the hills on the north side of Weno where today's top Chuukese students can get a first-rate education. The main structure is a former Japanese communications building with a reinforced concrete roof and walls four and five feet thick, impervious to direct hits during Operation Hailstone. Arthur Tewasiliig, the valedictorian of his class at the high school, was accepted at Northeastern University in Boston, Massachusetts.

Chuuk is in the Intertropical Convergence Zone (ITCZ) between the tropic of Cancer and the tropic of Capricorn. The Coriolis effect, an inertial force described by the 19th-century French civil engineer Gustave-Gaspard Coriolis, influences the weather, deflecting storm systems that turn to typhoons as they churn northward. This meteorological phenomenon means that when it rains, it usually doesn't rain for long, and you can generally expect

12 months of summer.

The morning weather was beautiful, sunny with puffy clouds and light seas. My computer cycled off indicating it had determined that I had reached my detoxicity level for residual nitrogen. My fellow divers said I had "off-gassed." I was looking forward to the next dives after the exciting sights on the *Hoki* and the *Fujikawa*.

The superstructure of the 395' *Seiko Maru* begins at 105 feet with the deck at 140'. Originally built for civilian cargo and passengers, its mission had changed under the command of the Japanese navy. It lies at the bottom of what was the Eten anchorage. I was the first one in the water that morning and swam to the wreck lying towards the west away from the boat. Usually our dive boat would swing on its mooring line. Aining would always go down first to set the line when the ship's bell rang. I swam about halfway down and headed for the torpedo hold to set my dive profile for the maximum depth first.

There was a 75mm field artillery gun mounted on the bow. I knew it was not the usual platform-mounted ship's gun since it had wheels, and a few wooden spokes remained. At the bow gun I saw a piece of coral shaped like a mask. A mollusk within the coral's eye closed its shell, simulating the ghostly winking of an eye. There were 24-inch diameter Long Lance torpedo bodies without warheads in the forward hold. Beams spaced evenly apart spanned the entrance to holds #1 and #5. It was curious to see what looked like coconut tree trunks and spoked wheels in one of the holds. Spare propellers were on the deck just forward of the funnel. There were companionways along the hull and I could see the galley with plates and bowls and their flag insignias. Other rooms contained tile bathtubs, urinals, and retrofit cabinets and storage compartments to make it suitable for the Japanese navy. It was a fairly deep dive, but at this point in the week we were accustomed to the complexities of wreck penetration.

Afterward, we motored out beyond the fringing reef to a spot on *Pizion Reef* for a spectacular shark-feeding session. The crew chummed with bloody fish parts, which attracted a large school of blacktip sharks (*Carcharhinus limbatus*) that churned the water before we entered. They were fast and agile, jumping over each

28

other on the surface to get at the bait. The sharks swam in a feeding frenzy, twisting their bodies as they attacked and competed for the available food. Much to our surprise, the blacktips were swimming in consort with gray reef sharks (*Carcharhinus amblyrhyncos*) and red snapper (*Lutjanus bohar*) off the stern dive platform. We were mystified as to why the snapper were there since they are not "cleaner" fish like remoras or other suckerfish. Red snapper is a featured "catch-of-the-day" in many seafood restaurants. Nevertheless, the sharks left them alone and went after the chum, ignoring the other fish including sweetlips and fusiliers. We saw this behavior repeated when Lenny set a single baitfish on a steel cable during our choreographed feeding on the reef below.

We wondered who would be the first to venture into the water. Paul, the commercial pilot I met on the flight from Houston, took the plunge and the rest of us quickly followed, swimming to the coral reef at a depth of about eighty feet. Lenny took an inflatable bag and attached it to a pulley. He lifted the bag, revealing the frozen bait tied securely to the steel cable anchored on the coral, and moved away while the exposed baitfish thawed. The sharks circled. Once the sharks got the scent, they converged and the scene quickly turned into a feeding frenzy as the sharks feverishly attacked the bait.

Two large female silvertips (*Carcharhinus albimarginatus*), along with a smaller male, gracefully surveyed the scene, biding their time for the right moment. Once the four to six foot blacktips and gray reef sharks had ample opportunity to tear and chew the bait, one of the wide body female silvertips accelerated into the scrum and muscled the bait free from the cable, swallowing it as she headed out into the blue water, while the others futilely tried to snatch it away from her.

The sharks were all around us, but they were averse to our exhalation bubbles. The scene repeated itself again at the second feeding session, only this time the big female silvertip violently bent the cable into a horizontal position with her formidable strength while ripping the mackerel free.

After it was over, I swam down to the base of the cable and found a shark's tooth. My dive knife came in handy since the tooth was partially hidden in a coral hole. I took off my gloves and used the serrated edge of the knife together with my forefinger to grab the tooth and extract it from its hiding place. I was afraid it would slip away out of my grip, but I managed to get it free. I carefully placed it in my dive glove as I ascended gingerly to the surface. I put it in a safe place: a hard-shell eyeglass case wrapped in a small plastic bag and protected by a soft cloth. Later, I mounted the tooth on a pendant as a memento of the thrilling experience.

The pelagic predators were not the only violent species in the history of Truk Lagoon. There were heinous crimes and atrocities committed during the Japanese occupation. After the war, tribunals were held resulting in the conviction of officers, enlisted men and civilians. The crimes were horrific. One witness testified to seeing downed American pilots suspended between coconut palms, where the Japanese used them for bayonet practice, after which they strangled the Americans if they were not already dead. Among the crimes were murders, torture, medical experiments, cannibalism, neglect of command duty, and other violations of customs of war. The focus of this book is not on war crimes, but these crimes came to the foreground in this context. Here is an account of the final moments of the last men executed:

> The last pair of twelve Japanese to die were to be Rear Admiral Shimpei Asano and Surgeon Cdr. Chisato Ueno. The code word "*Kobe*" was signaled to the stockade and the two men were taken from their cells and handcuffed with their arms behind their backs. They were escorted by Marine guards to a jeep code-named "Blue Boy" and taken the short distance to the quonset, where a Marine corporal waited to carry out his orders for execution. Upon entering the room, the condemned saw two rows of ten chairs for witnesses and officials
>
> Two 3/4" manila hemp ropes, twenty feet in length and treated with wax to insure a smooth sliding action, hung from the gallows. The specifications for the rope followed an English hangman's formula. In determining the length of the drop, the formula stated that the weight of the man to be hanged should be divided into the figure 840, and that the result was considered as the number of feet to which thirteen inches should be added. Tied on each rope was a knot known by hangmen as a clean loop sliding keeper. The front of the gallows was covered with heavy blue canvas to conceal the space beneath the trap door.

Chisato Ueno had been sentenced to death on February 17th, 1948, exactly four years to the day since the attack on Truk. Now, shortly after eight o'clock on the humid, tropical evening of March 31, 1949, according to War Department Pamphlet #27-4 Procedure for Military Executions, the 5' 6" Japanese surgeon with extremely strong neck muscles was escorted up the nine steps to the gallows. The handcuffs were removed by a Marine guard, and a strap placed to secure his arms to his side and another placed around his legs. A black hood was placed over his head and at 8:26 p.m. the floor panel on which he was standing fell from under his feet and Ueno dropped 94 inches to eternity. He was the last to die, as Rear Admiral Shimpei Asano had preceded him only moments before. Under the dubious honor that rank has its privileges - the Admiral went first.[3]

The *Rio de Janeiro* was a large 461' passenger and cargo liner, submarine tender and transport for troops and weapons. The wreck lies on its starboard side east of Uman Island where it was bombed on the port side facing east while anchored. The anchor was heavily encrusted with corals and surrounded with clusters of marine life. The hull was collapsed near the bow, deformed and bent inward, perhaps from a near miss. There was a large bow gun (six-inch; 50-caliber) in the sand. The bow and forecastle (foc'sle) contained exploded ammunition shells. Parts of the hull were pushed outward from these interior explosions. There was a hold with a rotating gun turret, two coastal defense guns, and coal. The cargo in the aft hold included intact cases of sake arranged like a ghostly wine rack with hundreds of bottles. A ship's telegraph rested on the stern deck. There were some exquisite pieces of china plates and rice bowls. The superstructure pilothouse contained magnificent large, long, enclosed passageways with tricky penetrations. I played with some large Tridacna clams in a cluster. Touching the shells made them close and I watched them open slowly. This was not a deep wreck; holds were around 80' deep, and the sandy bottom was 110'.

The only Betty Bomber in Truk Lagoon was next on our dive itinerary. This was a small wreck compared to the large ships we had already seen. The "Betty," as denoted by its allied nickname and codename, was actually a Mitsubishi G4M Navy Type 1 Attack Bomber, the most famous attack bomber built by Mitsubishi Jukogyo KK (Mitsubishi Heavy Industries Co.) beginning in

31

1940 as a replacement for the G3M Navy Type 96 Attack Bomber (codename "Nell"). It rests on the bottom in shallow water (63′ maximum depth) just southwest of Eten Island. The plane was made of metal with fabric control surfaces and three-blade propellers.

It must have been a violent crash because the two engines were far beyond the fuselage. I used a compass to find one engine at 110 degrees, and then returned by following the reverse heading of 290 degrees. My navigation was slightly off course and I had to make an adjustment, but I made it back to the *Odyssey* with plenty of air.

Ironically, Admiral Isoroku Yamamoto, the man who planned the attack on Pearl Harbor, was the Betty Bomber's chief advocate. Yamamoto was flying in a Betty Bomber when radio operators intercepted a coded message that he would be inspecting defenses in the Solomon Islands. Two U. S. Army Air Force pilots shot him down on April 18, 1943. Yamamoto was riddled with bullets in his aircraft seat. He was cremated and his remains were taken to Tokyo on the battleship *Musashi*. The *Musashi* was stationed at Truk from January 1943 until 1944 as part of the naval force guarding against the threat of an American offensive. When it became clear that attacks were on the way with an increase in allied reconnaissance flights over Truk, the *Musashi* sailed for Palau.

We had an excellent meal after the day's diving: shish kabob, rice, grilled tuna, corn pudding, and ice cream with chocolates and nuts for dessert. The day before, we had sashimi tuna for a mid-afternoon snack and that day we had lemon squares. I saw the Southern Cross constellation and Orion again that night in clear skies.

The deep dive we'd all been waiting for was the *San Francisco Maru*, often called the "Million Dollar Wreck." The former passenger/cargo ship rests perfectly on an even keel with major damage to the stern. It was very deep, resting on the bottom at 210′, far beyond the limits of sport diving, yet extremely exciting for experienced wreck divers. It was my deepest descent ever at 170 feet. Most of the Nitrox divers used air for this decompression dive; although a couple of holdouts insisted upon a 22% blend of oxygen (air is 21% O_2). Harty filled my 112 cu. in. tank with 3300 psi. We were divided into groups of five at staggered intervals. Each group descended down the mooring line in turn. Nitrox tanks were set up at safety intervals for the ascent.

Japanese Type 95 HA-Go light tank on *San Francisco Maru*
Credit: Photo by Jack Connick. Copyright 2003, Jack Connick Creative Services, Inc.

The *San Francisco* had fewer corals and less marine growth because of the depth. There is a beautiful bow gun. Hold #1 contained numerous hemispherical beach-type mines, munitions and densely stacked aerial bombs with boxes of cordite on the forward side shelves. Locals had taken some mines to use for now-illegal dynamite fishing. The ship's bell was taken in 1978.

Hold #2 contained several vehicles, tableware, drinking glasses, and mess kits. The most stunning sight was the three battle tanks, Type 95 HA-Go light tanks (manufactured by Mitsubishi), on the deck beside the hold. One of them rested intact on the deck. Two others overlapped on the foredeck either from the force of the explosion or when the ship hit the bottom.

Later, when I finally reached Peleliu, I saw the same model

tanks, rusted and without turrets, where they were stopped in an ill-fated attempt to defend the airfield from the Marines.

My Suunto Companion® dive computer automatically sets the decompression ceiling and time, then "barred out" to indicate it was time to ascend to the next level. I did three decompression stops at 30', 20' and 10'. The first two were brief, but the last didn't "bar out" until about eight minutes had passed. The dive computer never went into "DECO" mode and it was a safe, deep, and astonishing dive.

The *M.V. Truk Odyssey* is an extraordinary vessel amenitized with everything a technical diver could want. It is a comfortable ship with carpet and air conditioning throughout. Air tanks are filled where you sit, and you store your gear in compartments on the dive deck, a few steps from the dive platform. The ship was built in 1978 and refitted in 1999 in Louisiana. According to Captain Lenny, Naval Intelligence photographed the ship while transiting the Panama Canal. I asked about a charter, and the rate is reasonable at $23,500 a week for up to 12 divers.

Chuuk clearly presents an enormous opportunity for diving historic World War II wrecks filled with artifacts and weapons. The *S.S. Thorfinn*, the first dive liveaboard in Truk Lagoon, was originally constructed in Norway fifty years ago as an Ice Class Antarctic Whaler and then refitted as a charter cruiser in 1977. It anchors between Uman and Eten and remains stationary while four 24-foot dive boats transport six-person groups to the dive sites. The *Truk Aggressor*, built in 1988 and refitted in 2000, motors around the lagoon like the *Odyssey* to anchor directly over the wrecks. We spotted the ship a few times in the expansive waters strewn with underwater shipwrecks.

One day we were anchored between Dublon, where many people live including Harty the divemaster, and the island of Fefan within sight of Moen, where the Truk Airport is located. The other divers were exploring the *Heian Maru*, a submarine tender with periscopes, torpedoes, two warheads, shells and china. It is one of the largest ships in the lagoon. The ship's name is legible in English and Japanese on the bow and it means "Swallow Bird."

I observed many skiffs with 40 HP Yamaha outboards plying

34

the waters between the islands. These were the preferred modes of public transportation, a far cry from the old dugout canoes, although these boats did not have underwater emissions control and made a lot of noise. At times there were six to ten in the water transporting people between the islands. One skiff with three aboard tied up briefly at our stern, and the occupants spoke in Chuukese with our crew: Madison, Aining and Harty. Later, a single boat came out from the Blue Lagoon on Moen with one diver and a divemaster along with the boat operator. It made our luxury dive yacht seem extravagant. Lenny and Cara, our captains, told us they own and operate the ship. I had booked my trip through the *Odyssey's* Jacksonville office in Florida.

The *Truk Odyssey* is the best liveaboard in the lagoon according to the worldwide rankings in the diving industry. Everyone aboard agreed. Captains Lenny and Cara run a superlative operation. Harty is an expert divemaster who is a fantastic diving companion and guide. The cooks and deckhands are always working and eager to help. The divehands rinsed my fins and light and put them in my locker while I was still standing under the shower washing the rest of my gear. The wrecks are spectacular.

My last dive was the *San Francisco Maru* since I had to leave a day earlier than the rest of the divers to catch a flight to Yap, but it was a memorable dive to end this part of my journey.

The size of the lagoon certainly justifies the term "Pacific Gibraltar." There is ample evidence of the Japanese fortification and build-up of air and naval forces. The Japanese chose the location for its strategic advantage and natural features, a protected lagoon surrounded by reefs. The only time our boat went outside the reef was to feed the sharks.

Amelia Earhart, the first woman to pilot a non-stop flight across the Atlantic Ocean, and her navigator Frederick J. Noonan departed from Lae, New Guinea on July 2, 1937 headed for Howland Island, 1,650 miles southwest of Honolulu. It was a month since they had left Miami on their circumnavigation of the globe. Their flight path would have taken them northeast over the Carolines and the Marshall Islands. Workers on Howland Island had scrambled to prepare the airfield, but the flyers never arrived.

Today, the lighthouse on Howland is called the Amelia Earhart Light. Did she have enough fuel to divert her flight over Truk in order to photograph the military installations?

Looking back on the week, it seems that many of the divers were oblivious to the history; they were concerned more with cameras, housings, strobes, equipment, pictures, dive profiles and the diving itself as if Truk Lagoon was some sort of theme park for technical divers. At a glance, you would think the dive platform was a scuba diver's trade show with a multiplicity of double tank systems, dual isolation manifolds, valve yokes with redundant regulators, oxygen for decompression stops, re-breathers, pony bottles and reels.

However, when you contemplate the massive wrecks below the surface it is easy to see that Truk was a *Gunko*; a major naval base, and you realize that those cargo vessels were an integral part of the major supply lines for the Japanese forces in the Pacific. Admiral Mineichi Koga, who replaced Yamamoto as Commander-in-Chief of the Combined Japanese Fleet, ordered Admiral Kurita's 2nd Fleet to Palau and sent Vice Admiral Jisaburo Ozama's Carrier Fleet to Singapore. Koga steamed to Japan for approval to reorganize his navy deployments. He anchored in Tokyo on February 18, one day after the attack in Truk. Koga was unable to reverse the tide of the war and he was killed in a plane crash while retreating near Borneo in the spring of 1944.

If these ships at the bottom of Truk Lagoon had cleared the reef in early 1943, the battlefields on the islands on the way to Japan would have undoubtedly held additional lethal weapons against the allied forces, and the Marines storming the beaches. The submarine tenders *Rio de Janeiro* and *Heian*, the destroyer *Fumitzuki* and converted passenger freighters like the *Hoki*, *Fujikawa* and *San Francisco* were teeming with fresh supplies, heavy machinery, shore artillery guns, ammunition, torpedoes, military tanks, trucks, planes and bulldozers. It is difficult to imagine what these machines of war could have done, or how they might have changed the outcome of the war. Sinking these ship accomplished an important strategic objective, the destruction o a bastion that was an imminent danger to all of the forces in actio on the island route established by MacArthur and Nimitz. To call them cargo ships is a misnomer; they were military supply ships carrying weapons meant to supply enemy forces whose defense plan ordered to kill, destroy, annihilate and inflict the maximum number of casualties on the forces of the United States Army, Navy and Marine Corps.

Marines were captured and executed on Wake Island in December 1941. The island of Tarawa in the Gilberts saw the 2nd Marine Division take heavy casualties in a three-day battle to gain control of a strategic airstrip at Betio in November 1943. Tarawa was a pivotal battle, made especially difficult when the Japanese fortified the atoll (Betio) with long-range British-made shore guns. Over 1,000 Marines lost their lives in less than 72 hours. Virtually all of the amtrac (LVT)[4] personnel, perhaps 75 to 100 amtracs with 2 or 3 man crews, were either killed or wounded including Corporal Thomas Fenton Platt, Jr. (USMC), the brother of my friend Al Platt.

The amtracs were originally designed for use in the Florida Everglades and were manufactured by Food Machinery Corporation (FMC) in Lakeland and Dunedin. A unit of Marines trained in Dunedin and practiced landings on the small islands offshore in that area. Many LVTs on Tarawa were lost for lack of armor.

Assault troops also arrived on Higgins boats that became caught on the reef. The men had to go over the side 800 to 1,000 yards offshore and wade in with full combat packs on their backs with M-1 rifles held over their heads, facing the very intense automatic weapons fire of the Japanese. Each one of those men was a hero. Over 5,000 Japanese were killed.

Admiral Nimitz received a lot of criticism after Tarawa. Subsequently, many changes took place before future invasions. Two important decisions made as a result of the losses on Tarawa were to create underwater demolition teams (UDT) to recon the beaches before future assaults, and to remove the Higgins boats from duty and fortify the LVTs with more side armor. The lessons from the battle significantly helped Marine assault troops as they moved through the Marshalls (Kwajalein) just north of the Gilberts, the Solomons to the south (Guadalcanal, Cape Gloucester), and the islands from Western Micronesia (Guam, Peleliu) to Japan (Okinawa, Iwo Jima). In the Marshalls, Kwajalein was taken with fewer troop losses by the 4th Marine Division and Army soldiers in a brilliant campaign backed by significant naval and air bombardment thanks to the hard lessons learned at Tarawa. The 4th Marine Division and the Army's 7th Infantry took Eniwetok in June 1944.

The weather seemed to be building as I prepared to dry my gear in anticipation of flying to Guam and Yap the next day. After a week of spectacular and somber diving in the World War II graveyard of the Pacific, I had finally "off-gassed." My dive computer was in its normal mode without the SLOW or DECO warnings. The flashing airplane had shut off only once during this week. I took a long surface interval as a precautionary measure before departure.

Cara told me she'd take me to the airport at 12:30 P.M. and the rest of the guests would go ashore later to spend their evening at the Blue Lagoon. The farewell dinner onboard ship was a feast. The dining room was filled with the aromas of lobster tail, steak cooked to order, baked potato, and an apple crepe dessert. I had anticipated having French toast and bacon for breakfast the next morning, but it was just too much to eat.

After dinner we gathered in the ship's library/gift shop/media center where Cara showed the DVD video of our adventures. I purchased a copy to take back to Florida. The sea life was wondrous, the artifacts of humanity reminded us of the quotidian duties of life—eating, drinking, washing, shaving, personal hygiene and other bodily functions. Additionally, the shipwrecks tell another story—mortality, war, aggression, and the transitory fragile nature of life. The artifacts attested to the ferocious coastal defense strategy Japan intended to wage for the remainder of the Pacific War. There were the usual ship fittings: superstructure control rooms, helms and levers to telegraph "Full Speed Ahead" below decks to the engine room. Nearly every ship displayed evidence of bow or stern guns, bullets, shells and other weapons of war.

In 1969, Jacques Cousteau sponsored an expedition with nautical charts indicating wreck locations and to discover additional wrecks using side-scan sonar. They chartered a local ship and made the documentary film *Lagoon of Lost Ships*. The team discovered 18 "new" wrecks in addition to the 12 that had been identified previously. Kimiuo Aisek's memory of where the ships went down helped to find the major wrecks. The invention of side-scan sonar found the rest. Today there are between 38 and 42 wrecks to explore depending on the reference source, books or charts.

The Chuukese divemasters told me that the Cousteau group removed many artifacts in cargo containers. No one knows where the pieces are. They have not been put on display in the Cousteau Museum in Marseilles. Perhaps the family is deciding what to do with them. Members of the Cousteau Society have probably helped pay for warehouse storage. I asked Jacques Cousteau's grandson, Philippe, about the artifacts while diving with him in Bonaire on June 9, 2004. He is not affiliated with the Cousteau Society and did not realize that the artifacts existed or where they might be. His major concern is his foundation to conserve coral reefs.

It rained the day I left the *Odyssey*, and I couldn't take a good picture of my fellow divers gathered on the sun deck to wave goodbye as the skiff took me to Cara's waiting van at the Blue Lagoon Resort, and then to the airport. Captain Cara drove the van. We had a nice conversation while I videotaped the sights on the road to the airport including the Truk Stop Motel, stores, houses, schools and banks. By the time I arrived in Yap, the weather had turned into torrential rains across most of Micronesia, except for Truk. I felt somewhat responsible for bringing the weather north with me from Chuuk Lagoon.

Footnotes

[1] See Dan E. Bailey, *World War II Wrecks of the Truk Lagoon*, Redding, California: North Valley Diver Publications, 2000, for the exact locations of shipwrecks.

[2] Dan Bailey, *World War II Wrecks of the Truk Lagoon*, Boston: Little, Brown and Company, 2003, p. 309.

[3] William H. Stewart, *Ghost Fleet of the Truk Lagoon*, Missoula, Montana: Pictorial Histories Publishing Company, 1985, p. 105, 106. Excerpts from the *Final Report of the Navy War Crimes Program*.

[4] Landing Vehicle Tracked (LVT).

Yap 4

The intrepid traveler arrived in Yap after a brief stop in Guam from Chuuk. It was night in Yap, around 9:10 P.M., and we disembarked and headed for the immigration line where they checked our passports. A young woman greeted us at the airport after clearing the checkpoint. She was wearing a grass skirt and a necklace of flowers. Bare breasts are the custom in the local villages, although it is taboo for tourists, or any local woman, to wear short shorts or a mini-skirt. Although I knew this was the custom, I was somewhat surprised to see a topless young woman at the gate placing a floral wreath upon my head. Surprised, but not shocked, as the travel books and my father's stories had prepared me for it.

The baggage claim was crowded due to the small holding area, and after the bags arrived I went through customs behind Bill Raynor, whom I had met in the waiting lounge at the Guam airport. He went through without a problem, but the official inspecting my bags seemed mystified by my Leki® retractable trekking staff. The officer had a wide smile while chewing betel nut, a popular habit throughout Micronesia. It stained his teeth, tongue, gums and mouth the color of Ocean-Spray® cranberry juice. I suggested that he lean on the stick to feel the soft anti-shock mechanism and experience its utility for walking. That satisfied his curiosity and we moved out to the waiting vans.

Bill Raynor is director of The Nature Conservancy for Micronesia and was in Yap for a conference. The Nature Conservancy works with local groups and governments to develop educational programs and takes a proactive approach to environmental conservation and protection. Dedicated people like Bill and his colleagues will keep these islands in as close to a pristine state as possible, protecting fragile ecosystems and creating public awareness of important issues pertaining to the ecosystem and land use planning. Yap is a member of the Federated States of Micronesia (FSM). The island has an area of 39 square miles and a population of 11,500. Unlike many other islands in the Pacific, Yap is part of the Asian Continental Shelf, surrounded by a long and wide barrier reef.

I called my parents at the Temple Terrace house in Florida around 11:30 P.M., which was 8:30 A.M. in Florida after taking the fifteen-hour time difference into account. They weren't home and I called my sister to let her know my whereabouts and my adventures in Chuuk.

I intended to take a walk and shoot some photographs of the area, including the place my father landed and the hill he climbed in 1945. He described it as a harbor with a steep hill nearby. The Manta Ray Bay Hotel in Colonia, the capital city, overlooked the main harbor. I knew the hill couldn't be very far away

I scheduled a land tour to see and hear the local performances consisting of story telling and narrative dance. One aspect of my research concerned the displacement and performance traditions of indigenous people, and how war had disrupted and affected their lives as reflected in pre- and postwar performance traditions. Yap is a fertile area for study, as it is visited by fewer tourists than Palau, probably a tenth of the number who visit Palau in a year. It provides a unique opportunity for time-travel. The young woman in traditional dress handing out flower wreaths in the airport reinforces the notion of a way of life that no longer exists on most of the other islands in the Federated States of Micronesia.

The hotels and restaurants are as modern as any in the western Pacific islands, yet many Yapese live in isolated villages with government-controlled access, sheltered from the encroachment of modern culture. The people are encouraged to maintain their traditional lifestyle. The dances of Yap tell stories about the history of the island. Nevertheless, the people have long lost the memory of the reasons why they perform. However, as the dances are transmitted from one generation to the next, the children learn about their own ancient heritage. There are four types of dances: 1.) The bamboo dance; 2.) The marching dance; 3.) The sitting dance; and 4.) The standing dance. Men and women perform the sitting and standing dances separately.

Fathann was the name of the mythical ancient navigator who discovered the limestone of Palau and returned to Yap with the first stone money. Originally quarried and finished in the shape of a crescent moon, it evolved into a circular stone carved in a donut-like shape of varying sizes with a hole in the middle. Since the stone money is heavy and difficult to carry, the hole would make it easier to transport using a log or branch of a tree. Carbon dating has placed some of the older stones back 1,500 to 2,000 years ago. The stones are actually crystalline calcite, a marble-like material. Stone money is still used today in the villages, and each village has an area with piles of stones in an outdoor bank. Surprisingly, Yap Divers, the dive operator at the Manta Ray Bay Hotel, had stone money in the courtyard near their boat dock.

The value of the large stones is based upon several factors: the quality of the calcite, its size and shape, and the tools and quarrying techniques. The most important element is the history of the particular stone's transportation from Palau. Without NOAA weather forecasts, the journey could be treacherous and deadly. The difficulty of the journey and how many lives were risked in order to bring the stone to Yap are determining factors in the valuation of a particular stone. One piece over 250 lbs. is considered the most valuable because of the number of men who perished during the delivery.

I awakened at 6:23 A.M. and it was still dark. The first order of business was to go down to the dive shop to show them my certification card and sign the waiver form. The two main diving questions in my mind had to do with buoyancy compensation for the 3000-psi 80-cubic-foot aluminum tank, much lighter than the steel 112 in Chuuk, and whether I could take the Nitrox certification course. Another question, not diving-related, was where my father was on Yap during his second tour of duty in Micronesia when he was among the first Marines to "sanitize" the islands and dispose of enemy ordnance. I did not realize in the torrential rains that he performed one of his duties within sight of where I was staying at the Manta Ray Bay Hotel. I never saw the sun or blue sky the entire time I was in Yap. The constant precipitation and low-ceiling cloud cover obscured the peak of my father's hill for the first couple of days.

Breakfast was in the *Mnuw*, a replica pirate ship moored in the channel behind the hotel. A nice young man named Jeremiah shook my hand when I told him I was an American and my father was in Yap with the Marines in 1945. The food was good, and I had a hearty bacon, cheese and mushroom omelet with toast and hot tea.

Although the dive boats go out rain or shine, and I saw Bill Raynor, the TNC Director, preparing to dive on his only free morning before his environmental and educational conference, the torrential downpour and correspondingly poor visibility made me decide to skip the morning dives and take the Nitrox course. I stowed my gear in a locker at the dive shop.

Freddie, the dive shop manager who smoked constantly, handed me a book along with tables for RDP (recreational dive planning) and a video for EANx (Enriched Air Nitrox). After the week of endless diving among the ghost ships of Truk Lagoon, it was a welcome respite to take a day off and study for Nitrox certification while waiting for the weather to clear. Nitrox would give me an extra margin of safety, extending my no-decompression limits, but I knew there were tradeoffs. As the saying goes, "There's no such thing as a free lunch."

The air we breathe consists of two main gases: nitrogen (79%) and oxygen (21%). EANx blends extend from 22% to 40% oxygen. Essentially, the nitrogen in a tank of compressed air for diving is replaced with a higher percentage of oxygen, reducing the residual nitrogen that builds up in the bloodstream. This helps to reduce, but not eliminate the potential for DCS (decompression sickness).

In addition to these advantages, there are a few disadvantages to diving with Nitrox blends. Nitrox has a greater potential for fire or explosion with its higher oxygen content. Smoking while you are using the oxygen analyzer before your dive could be very hazardous to your health. You must analyze the percentage of oxygen in your tank in order to determine your no-decompression limits, EAD (equivalent air depth) and MOD (maximum overall depth) with a particular Nitrox blend. If you make a mistake and exceed the MOD, you could suffer the consequences of oxygen toxicity, a serious and immediate danger. The symptoms may include blurred vision, nausea, twitching, irritability, or dizziness. Additionally, there are strict protocols for obtaining enriched air fills.

I called Mom and Dad the next morning using my AT&T calling card. It was a clear connection and I told them where I was and my adventures up to that point in the trip. They were pleased to hear from me. When I asked how things were going with them, they said the house and yard were O.K., but the lawn and pool care service hadn't shown up yet. I told them I could barely see a hill above the sea wall and road behind the hotel. Dad mentioned that he blew up a large gun emplacement on the summit overlooking the harbor. I looked on the map and it is the highest peak on the island at 147 feet, right next to the waterfront and main harbor.

I met several travelers and residents at breakfast the next morning in the *Mnuw*. Mike and Chris, a couple from Colorado, were here for two days before taking the infrequent flier: the small Pacific Missionary Aviation plane that takes passengers to Ulithi. I made a special effort to meet Bill Acker, the owner of the hotel. He used to work for the Peace Corps years ago and subsequently decided to stay and found the recreational diving industry on Yap. Captain Cara from the *Truk Odyssey* had asked me to give him her regards.

I met Maria, a new employee hired to develop a video and photo center, while I wandered around the hotel lobby looking for T-shirts and souvenirs. Originally from Great Britain, she had recently moved from Grand Cayman, B.W.I. after receiving the job offer with Yap Divers. Coincidentally, I had worked extensively with Henry and Marcia Muttoo of the Cayman Cultural Foundation and also dived many of the extraordinary reefs and walls of Grand Cayman and Cayman Brac for the past twenty years. Maria had

45

been to a traditional Yapese village performance the day before I arrived. She showed me the raw digital footage on her Mac. It was colorful and sharp. Although she was in the process of setting up her shop, I asked her if I could purchase a copy because my own prospects for a village visit were less than optimistic due to the weather. She said when it was ready she would mail me a DVD. I resolved to keep my fingers crossed and contact her through the hotel's website when I got back to Tampa. Anyway, it was time to get back to the books and video for the Nitrox exam.

Later that day, after a long session of studying and solving math problems, the rain clouds cleared briefly at dusk, and a higher hill appeared just above the one I noticed above the sea wall. It had been shrouded in the mist, but now I could see three radio and terrestrial microwave towers at the peak. That must have been where Dad destroyed the shore artillery installed by the Japanese to protect the harbor. I doubted whether I would climb it in the rainy conditions, or whether there was any debris up there, but the locals told me that it was the highest peak protecting an anchorage suitable for freighters and larger ships.

The rain afforded me the opportunity to learn the material for Nitrox certification. Mike and his wife Chris had waited for two days of cancellations of their flight to Ulithi. They would wait for yet another day. My own search became easier the next morning.

The hotel room had a radio and television, but lacked program stations. You could watch VHS videotape, and I viewed the Nitrox training film while studying and learning the formulas for EAD (Enriched Air Depth), MOD (Maximum Overall Depth) and PO_2 (Partial Pressure of Oxygen) expressed in absolute atmospheres (ata). Most dive operations feature two Nitrox blends: EANx 32 or EANx 36 with the number standing for the percentage of oxygen. However, the *Truk Odyssey* provided a wider range and the majority of divers opted for EANx 28 with a PO_2 of 1.4 ata.

The third day on Yap was much like the first two. The rain came down in sheets, briefly subsided, and poured again. It cleared somewhat the day before, but not enough to see any blue sky. It didn't matter because I passed my Nitrox exam with a perfect

46

score and decided to dive at 9 A.M. regardless of how much it rained. My father had recommended that I bring a lightweight water-resistant jacket and pants because he knew the rains could come up unexpectedly in the dry season. That was the first time and place I needed them and they were perfect for the weather conditions. I still wanted to get that picture of Dad's hill in Yap near the hotel, but I doubted I would be able to climb it to see what was up there.

I had signed up for the Tuesday evening cultural tour to a Yapese village where I would see dancing, weaving and piles of stone money, but unless five more people signed up, the tour operator would cancel. Later in the afternoon, I walked up to Traders' Ridge, a hotel across the street, following a path behind O'Keefe's Bar & Grille near the police station and land offices, where I learned they would take as few as two guests on the village tour. The only thing standing in the way was the rainy weather.

Finding my father's hill was made easy by a chance encounter at breakfast in the *Mnuw*. It began with another pleasant conversation with Mike and Chris from Colorado. They were upbeat despite being stuck on Yap and were anxious to check on the status of their flight, hoping to be headed to Ulithi that day on the missionary plane for their planned dive on a remote and pristine reef.

Cathy, the waitress on the docked pirate ship/restaurant, told me she was originally from Ulithi. I asked permission to record an interview with her. She consented and showed me a USNR dog tag she had found in her taro patch on the island of Mogmog. She said they were digging in the earth when they discovered the dog tag with the name Harold Gordon. She wanted to find his family and return it. He was most likely a Seabee (CB), reinforcing my admiration for the work done by the U. S. Navy's construction battalions, as they were instrumental in restoring airfields and infrastructure on Yap, Ulithi and particularly on Peleliu.

I showed Cathy from Mogmog my father's USMC dog tag and told him he was on Yap and Ulithi in 1945 disposing ordnance and blew up a big shore artillery gun protecting the harbor while sanitizing the island. She told me that her own father was forced to be a spotter for the Japanese, and described how he fell from a coconut palm high on the hill above us on Yap when an allied plane flew low above his head. He bears the scar to this day. It must be the same hill my father had climbed.

Hill with radio towers above the harbor in Colonia, Yap.
(Photo © 2004 Patrick Finelli)

My father told me about his duty on Ulithi and Yap:

My weight stabilized at Aiea Heights Hospital in Hawaii after I recovered from Peleliu. I took part in duty on shore patrol, but wanted to rejoin my original outfit. I was given orders and hitched a ride to the Marine airbase Ewa in Pearl Harbor. I flew to Johnson's Island, Kwajalein, Eniwetok and Guam. I heard that my outfit was in the Philippines. I noticed the markings of my unit while flying into Ulithi, and had them drop me off at the Headquarters of Marine Air Group 45, providing cover for the fleet as we pressed toward Japan.

I went back to my old job in bomb disposal. Our assignment was to clear the debris of war. After Okinawa, the Kamikazes made their desperate attempt to stop us, but many bombs were left unexploded on the ships. An LST was brought to Ulithi, and we had to salvage

48

equipment, clear bodies and remove explosives to make it safe. We anchored to one side and defused several bombs.

After the A-bomb, we had to go down and clear the island of Yap for the military government. The Japanese wouldn't tell us where the mines were. I was injured from shrapnel in Yap while performing clearing demolition duty. I returned stateside by hospital ship from Guam. My first stop back in the states was at Oak Knoll hospital in Oakland. Then I went by hospital train to the Chelsea Naval Hospital in December 1945, where I underwent an operation.[1]

During the conversation with Cathy from Mogmog, I noticed another guest eating his breakfast. I introduced myself and he replied that his name was Marty Hicks. He came to Micronesia for a few months each year with FEMA (Federal Emergency Management Agency) distributing food to the islands. Marty was a retired fire marshal and Vietnam vet. He had come from Falalop, another island on my father's tour of duty. There are over 30 islands in the Ulithi Atoll. Falalop had enough land for an airstrip and Marines. The Japanese had forced all of the local residents of Falalop to leave during the war. Asor, a small island nearby, housed administration and operations. Mogmog was where the Marines and sailors went for recreation. Other islands were used for ship repair. A few were the exclusive domains of the local tribes. Most of them retained their ancient traditions then as they continue to do today.

Dad told me that he disposed of tons of 1,000 and 500-pound bombs, torpedoes and other munitions in the islands of Ulithi. He and his unit loaded them into trucks, drove them onto pontoon boats, and took them out into channel between Falalop and Asor, where they sent them to the bottom along with other weapons and machinery, including planes. Dr. Paul Wees recounted the sounds of the demolition squads: "All through the early afternoon the blasts continued to shake us...They're just blasting out a new entrance to the lagoon."[2] I made a note to dive that area in the future to see if I could find what remained in that channel.

Marty Hicks offered to send me copies of *Life* magazines with Tom Lea's color drawings from the Battle of Peleliu (June 11, 1945) and another with a pre-invasion feature about Palau (April

24, 1944). He gave me his card with his e-mail address. Marty was very kind to send three copies of the magazines within a couple of weeks of my return home.

After breakfast, I went up to my room to get a clear dive mask (without color-correcting lenses) before heading over to the dive shop. I brought it along primarily for night dives, but it would help to see well in poor visibility. I was excited about the prospects of diving with Nitrox in the open water.

The weather was overcast, but the rain had ceased long enough for us to dive a wall outside the fringing reef. It was surprising to see Mike and Chris get on the boat because I knew they must be disappointed that their flight was cancelled again. My next flight in a couple of days would be only 50 minutes to Koror in the Republic of Palau. Continental Micronesia could fly when the missionary plane couldn't.

William, the boat driver, and Matthias, the deck hand and navigator, took us through German Channel, a small narrow passage through the mangroves, and then out into gentle 4-ft. swells without cresting and into the water for a smooth drift dive along the wall. We spotted seven lobsters in a coral outcropping under a rock. A couple of them were huge. We also saw a green turtle. Steve, a fellow from Washington's San Juan Islands and the only other diver with Nitrox, snapped several pictures.

After a one-hour surface interval, we went to the Manta Ray feeding station in the Mi'il Channel. Steve had worked in the nuclear industry at the Hanford, Washington Plutonium Finishing Plant (PFP) and enthralled us with tales about the handling of nuclear material. He told us of worker Harold McCloskey contaminated with americium in 1976 after an accidental chemical explosion inside a glove box sprayed his face with the largest dose of radiation ever recorded. It was the first use of the Hanford decontamination facility. McCloskey is identified as the "Atomic Man" in the October 1983 issue of *Health Physics*. He survived and became the subject of many detailed radiation studies. Reportedly his face could trigger Geiger counters 50 feet away. Amazingly he lived only to die of a heart attack eleven years later. You never know what you might hear from your dive buddies while motoring to the next site.

On the second dive a few of us saw a beautiful manta ray. It swam close to us, but many of the other divers were too far away to see it. The gorgeous, graceful creature was swimming effortlessly from the reef out to the deep. We saw a huge hump-headed parrotfish, which looks very similar to a large Napoleon wrasse. Trevally and colorful anemone fish completed the picture. The visibility was not as good as the first dive in the morning, but the Nitrox diving went fine and I looked forward to completing the written review for my "Enriched Air Diver" card.

The rain stopped for a while, and I walked up the path to the restaurant at Traders' Ridge after Steve's resounding recommendation of the lobster linguine. Steve and his wife Cindy were the only ones in the restaurant. I sat down with them and we ordered the last of the lobster. The food was delicious with plenty of iced tea and fresh bread. I told them about the reasons for my journey to Peleliu. They showed me their room and Steve loaned me a book he purchased in Koror titled *Peleliu Remembered* by Ann Owens Gilliland. It was a brief, 94-page paperback. Just in case it is not generally available, I have reprinted the poem that ends the book:

The Tears of Peleliu

On an island far out at sea,
The Pacific that is, where else could it be?
The Japs were there, we wanted that isle,
The Marines would take it in Leatherneck style.
The Navy and Air Force blasted the shore,
Then they hit 'em again with a lot more.
The First Marines were ready for a fight,
They would battle the Japs with all their might.
The Nips were dug in, they were determined to stay,
But they underestimated Company "K."
Well, the Marines stormed in all the way to the shore,
That was September 15, 1944.

51

A terrible price was paid to secure,
The island of Peleliu we know for sure.
In just three days the island was taken,
Except for Bloody Nose, the Japs wouldn't be shaken.
The dead and the wounded lay in the hot sun,
It just seemed the Japs would not run.
We often wonder as we mull in our heads.
Which was worse, killing or burying the dead.
It was an event we will never forget.
How some of us survived is a mystery yet.
Bloody Nose was taken, the Japs were beat,
In spite of the losses and terrible heat.
So back to Pavuvu and our homemade "privies,"
Where we did our chores and washed our "skivvies."
Now some are gettin' old and move kinda slow,
But we remember Peleliu, don't you know.
As we think back over the many years,
It wasn't all blood and sweat,
There were lottsa tears.

Eugene Stramel,
"Halftrack"
U.S. Marine

Steve and I were the only divers for my last day in Yap. The other divers wanted to go to the southern reefs, but the winds were out of the north and would make the return trip longer. I preferred to stay near the harbor since my flight to Palau was early the next day. A diver's body needs time to dissolve the residual nitrogen before flying, whether breathing Nitrox or not. We did two dives, the Mi'il Channel Manta Ray Feeding Station where we saw just one ray in poor visibility, and at a site called 122 at the entrance of the harbor. There, the diving was better than we expected. We saw lobster, moray, pipefish (related to sea horses), a turtle and a long sea slug with tentacles on its head. There was a whitetip shark, one of several we saw in Yap waters. The whitetip's body is much narrower than the silvertips in Chuuk. We spotted a unique creature I had never seen before—a mantis shrimp. It lived in a sand mound with an opening. Our divemaster, John, used a stick to lure it out. It looked like the monster in the movie *Alien* when it opened its jaws to snap the stick. It could have easily chomped on the finger of an unsuspecting diver, and uses the subterfuge of the sand pile to ambush its prey. Generally, the visibility was between twenty and thirty feet, but it did not rain while we were out on our two Nitrox dives.

After rinsing my gear and hanging it up to dry, I went up to Traders' Ridge for the cultural tour. It was delayed, and then cancelled due to rain. The heavens opened up and it poured during the late afternoon. At least I could hope it might clear up by the time I get to Palau. The Colorado couple, Mike and Chris, finally made their flight on the old missionary puddle-jumper.

The hotel desk clerk suggested I leave at 6:30 A.M. the next morning for the trip to the airport. She took my yellow immigration form, but I asked for and received a photocopy. I spread out all of my dive gear in the room to dry under the ceiling fans. I gave my e-mail address to Maria, the video specialist, so that she could send me the DVD with the dances and cultural activities, and perhaps even a few shots of the mantas.

I was ready to say so long to Yap. I never saw the sun or sky, but enjoyed the diving, the Nitrox and seeing one of my father's wartime hills.

Footnotes

[1] Personal interview with Patrick L. Finelli, June 17, 2002.

[2] Paul Marshall Wees, M.D., *King-Doctor of Ulithi*, New York: The Macmillan Company, 1950, p. 92.

Palau 5

I arrived in Koror early on St. Patrick's Day after a 45-minute flight from Yap. Jojo picked me up in the van at the airport to take me to the West Plaza Hotel on the island of Malakal. I was his only passenger. I asked him if he knew Tangie Hesus.

He said, "Yes, he is my friend. I'm picking him up tonight with a group returning from Peleliu. If you wait in the lobby of the hotel at around 5 P.M., you will meet Tangie. He is staying there." Tangie was with the Military Historical Tours group.

I was overjoyed. I had a difficult time getting in touch with Tangie. I had received only one e-mail message from him in reply to my many messages. Jojo's news was exciting and brought me closer to my goal. I made a mental checklist to be sure and bring my digital video camera and the Tampa Bay Buccaneer game day jersey with "Tangie" and the number "1" on the back to the lobby. My parents had given me a new pair of Reeboks as a present for Tangie. Everett Pope suggested the idea of bringing gifts when I spoke with him on the telephone back in Florida.

The day had started inauspiciously in the dark misty morning on Yap, but it was getting brighter and clearer by the minute on Palau. The waiting area at the Yap airfield was more like a holding cell than anything else, although I can't say I wasn't warned. Five of the divers on the *Truk Odyssey* had a layover in Yap on their way from Palau to Truk, the opposite direction to my own route. They described it as a crowded jail. I have to admit it had some jail-like features. The enclosure was relatively small, surrounded with concrete block walls and steel bars extending to the ceiling above. It was not air-conditioned, but open to the elements through the bars. All passengers, including those waiting for the flight to Palau and those in transit and required to deplane before re-boarding, had to remain in those cramped quarters until the announcement to board the plane. The fellows on the *Odyssey* were on the mark with their observations.

Although you could see the area surrounding the main building at the Yap airport, there were mostly elder Yapese women and children in traditional dress—grass skirts and topless.   Some tourists posed for pictures showing the locals in the background through the chain link fence as we walked on the tarmac to the stair ramp.

The Yapese women and family members had come to say goodbye to a male relative. The poor fellow kept wandering in and out of immigration and security lines in a constant state of confusion. The scene was repeated when we arrived in Koror and rather comical when you think of what would have happened if he acted the same way at Boston's Logan Airport or LAX.

Despite the inconvenience, I was philosophical about it since I knew what to expect. I eagerly anticipated the hour flight and was patient about finally getting to my ultimate destination. I had a pleasant conversation with a young Japanese-American woman named Yokiko while waiting for the flight to Palau from Yap. She worked as a dolphin trainer at Sea World of the Pacific, and was heading to Koror to visit her boyfriend for a few weeks.   She laughed and smiled knowingly when I mentioned that I would be diving with Sam's Tours in Malakal, since she might dive with Sam's as well.   I saw her boyfriend pick her up at the airport after we cleared the gate checkpoints in Palau. They crossed together into the parking lot while I waited for Jojo to bring the van around. Little did I know at the time that he was a divemaster at Sam's and would later introduce me to the best wall dive in the world—Blue Corner.

Immigration and customs at the Koror airport in the Republic of Palau were very efficient. The customs official engaged me in conversation and I told him about my father's Marine Corps experience on Peleliu back in 1944. He shook my hand as I went through the line.

The drive from the airport in Babeldoap took us through the commercial district of Koror and the more industrial island of

Malakal. We crossed the Japanese-Palau Friendship Bridge, a suspension bridge between the islands. Downtown Koror was dominated by Japanese culture, teeming with sushi restaurants, acupuncture clinics, karaoke bars and stores. I saw the main government offices, the Supreme Court and the Congress. The latter is in the former Japanese administration building. The vistas towards the water were stunning, with fantastic Rock Islands and bits of blue sky indicating the stormy weather from the low pressure system in Yap was clearing out.

Checking into the West Plaza was effortless as Jojo had radioed ahead and then carried my bags up to the room. It was time to unpack and walk over to Sam's dive shop. Much to my chagrin, torrential rains hit exactly when I was ready to go. The storm system wasn't done with me yet. Undaunted, I put on my rain gear and walked in the downpour a few hundred yards down to the dock to fill out the forms and show my certification cards at the dive shop.

Most of my contact with Sam's Tours prior to the trip had been with Russelle Caraig, an outstanding tour coordinator and manager. She is a true professional and helped me immensely during the planning phase of the trip. It didn't end there as Russelle's extraordinary talents and communication skills made many things possible before, during and after diving with Sam's.

There were two sociable and helpful young ladies working behind the counter named Irene and Maggie. Maggie was a blonde American from Sacramento, California, who told me she came to Palau and married Jonathan, a Palauan and a divemaster with Sam's. Maggie was born three years before I was certified as an open water diver. We chatted as the storm passed. There was no one else in the shop when I walked in soaking wet, but soon I saw a lot of divers milling around outside, rinsing gear after returning from the morning dive excursion. I went out for a moment to speak with a fellow whom I remembered from the flight several days earlier, during the leg between Guam and Yap. He sat next to me on the plane and mentioned he was headed to Palau. He had been diving with Sam's for two weeks. I asked him how he was doing and he said the weather had been rainy with choppy seas, but Blue Corner was worth it.

Sam Scott, the owner of Sam's Tours, moved to Palau from Olympia, Washington when his stepfather asked him to become the heir apparent to his position as chief (*Ibbedul*) of Koror, a powerful position in the ancient clan.

While Maggie and I were talking about the weather and scuba diving, in walked the boyfriend of the woman I met on the morning flight from Yap. Maggie called him Scott and I greeted him with a warm hello. He seemed taken aback that I knew his name and his girlfriend Yokiko. As fate would have it, he was scheduled to lead the next day's dive, although he wanted to take the day off.

Russelle worked out a schedule where I would dive three times the next day, two in the morning and one at night, then two dives on Friday. If the weather cooperated and the low-pressure system headed toward the Philippines, it would be a sunny day with little wind. In that case, Sam's dive boat would bring me to the Ngemelis wall for the last dive of the day, and either drop me off on Peleliu or the boat from the Storyboard Resort would pick me up from the island of Ngemelis (pronounced "Ge-meh-lees"). I'd do the rest of the dives after returning from Peleliu the next week.

I planned to bring just a knapsack and briefcase from Malakal to Peleliu. The items in my backpack included my trekking staff strapped to the outside, the HID dive light with a diffusion lens for illuminating caves, a Swiss Army knife, a GPS unit for accurately locating the position of battle sites and artifacts, a digital video camera, binoculars, a snapshot camera, bottles of water and Gatorade, a personal hygiene kit with prescriptions for Clarinex and Cipro, a spare pair of waterproof National Geographic shoes for the beaches to go with my National Geographic hiking shoes on the limestone hills, spare shorts, shirts, socks, and underwear. My briefcase held my wallet, passport, maps, notes, iPAQ Pocket PC, and money. Peleliu is a "cash-only" island and the U.S. dollar is the local currency. I planned to wear a safari hat, SPF lightweight shirt, and blue jeans. The water resistant jacket and pants and a "bug shirt" rounded out the attire for the 21st century battlefield explorer. I kept the room at the West Plaza on Malakal for stowing my dive gear and the rest of my luggage. I wanted to travel light to Peleliu and be able to move around without toting a lot of gear. I had worn my father's dog tag since I left Chuuk and intended to leave it behind on Peleliu at the end of my visit.

The primary art form in the Republic of Palau is the storyboard. Reputedly, the prisoners at the jail in Koror make the best ones, and the price depends on your ability to negotiate and the woodcarving skill of the artist. I decided to wait until my return for souvenir shopping.

My room at the West Plaza Malakal was excellent, comparable to the room at the Manta Ray Bay Hotel in Yap, spacious and clean. The hotel in Yap had a seating area with a couch and chairs. The bath, shower and toilet were in a separate room from the sink and countertop. The West Plaza Malakal combined the two into one bathroom. The sign over the spout on the sink warned, "Do not drink the water." Since I had to brush my teeth, it was a good idea to start a daily regimen of Cipro. The West Plaza had plenty of floor space, a balcony, two beds and a television that featured BBC Asia and the STAR Sports channels. United States basketball is very popular in Palau and Yap. I never quite became accustomed to the Japanese cooking shows or watching European rugby and billiard matches without commentary.

There were two grocery stores nearby, larger than convenience stores but nothing like Publix or Safeway in the States. One was small with a limited selection of items and higher prices. The other was the West Mini Mart, part of a grocery store chain. It was well stocked and the store clerk placed a sticker for a lottery drawing on each receipt. I picked up some bottles of water and Gatorade to put in the refrigerator in my room, and some pistachio nuts for a snack. The van from Sam's would arrive at eight in the morning, but I knew I'd be up long before then. Besides, I was looking forward to meeting Tangie that evening at long last when he returned from Peleliu with the military tour group.

I went down to the hotel lobby at the appointed hour. Tangie walked in and worked the room like a celebrity entertainer. He had an effervescent personality. The members of the tour group seemed tired. They had taken the public boat back from Peleliu. None were Peleliu battle veterans, although a few had served in the Marines and one Navy vet was a submariner. Their tour director, Jim Pilkington, seemed to be somewhat irritable as a few members aired some complaints about the organization of their trip. The men on the tour, and one woman named Diane Kuebler from Brookline, Massachusetts who had taken part in these Pacific battle site tours for the past three years, were extremely nice to me, with a couple of exceptions, and willing to tell me about their Peleliu tour despite their fatigue. More than a few wanted to go back again after they realized how many artifacts were there. Pilkington told me on camera that he wanted to find an artillery target grid map for Peleliu to complete his collection. Evidently, he laminated the maps. My father told me every company commander had one.

Tangie Hesus, Peleliu battlefield guide extraordinaire, was surprised and happy when I presented him with the gifts and we posed for pictures taken by Lisa, the desk clerk at the West Plaza. He was bubbling over with enthusiasm and invited me to come along with the group for dinner at an excellent Indian restaurant, The Taj. We piled into vans and stopped at a department store called Ben Franklin for T-shirts and souvenirs. As is the case with most tours, the fast shoppers had to wait for the slow ones, and we made it to the restaurant only about a half-hour late. All of them were taking the 2:30 A.M. Continental Airlines flight to Guam, but I had a dive scheduled for early in the morning. Several of us were anxious to get to dinner and back to the hotel.

The décor at The Taj made me feel like I was in India. Murals on the walls depicted traditional Indian scenes. The pleasant scent of curry wafted from the kitchen, visible through a window at the end of our table for twelve. We watched the pastry chef preparing *nan* bread, kneading the dough and then placing it into a device that looked like a flat waffle iron next to the traditional clay oven called a *tandoori*. *Nan* is soft flatbread suitable for picking up floating bits of curried chicken, shrimp and lamb. We could see the other chefs and assistants in the busy kitchen behind the *nan* chef's station.

The meal itself was superb, an extraordinary dining experience. The service was prompt and courteous; the presentation of the eleven-course meal was elegant and the food simply delicious. It began with light, nacho-like chips with tasty dip, salad, *nan* bread, and appetizer portions of shrimp and chicken. This was followed with soup, then several curries with chicken, shrimp and tender lamb blended with spices, herbs and ginger. Another course featured saffron-marinated chicken shish kabob skewered with tomatoes, sweet pepper, and more. Our hosts served fruit-covered ice cream as a palate-cleansing dessert. We agreed it was a delight and could have stayed there until dawn. Robert, the owner, had welcomed us when we arrived and we thanked him as we filed out to the parking lot at the end of the meal. It was an extraordinary gastronomic treat, a gourmet's dream. However, despite the delectable food, Tangie had some difficulty with this wonderful meal, and at every meal, since he is a vegetarian and the Palauan cuisine features a lot of chicken, meat and fish.

Two government ministers joined us for dinner. One was a member of the Governor's staff; the other was Temmy L. Shmull, Minister of State for the Republic of Palau. He was an articulate spokesman for his land and its people, a true gentleman as well as a charismatic public official. He handed me his business card and suggested I get in touch with him if I needed anything in Palau. Politely, I resisted the temptation to draw a connection with our own Secretary of State, Colin Powell and refrained from referring to him in good spirit as "Colin Palau."

Diane Kuebler, the daughter of an Iwo Jima Seabee, sat across from me and to her left was John Edwards, a 3rd Marine Division Vietnam war veteran. John was very helpful in explaining the technicalities of the ordnance used in the Battle of Peleliu. He said the United States forces employed a 2.36-inch rocket launcher during World War II known by its more familiar name of bazooka, and it was used on Peleliu. John knew a lot about weapons from his Marine service and expertise in military history.

He exclaimed, "It was an effective anti-tank weapon and very handy for caves and bunkers. I got to fire the 3.5" follow-on version in the 1960s and they are a real hoot."

Doug Meny, a pleasant chap from Palm Harbor in Florida, was at the head of our end of the table. Doug was an avid runner and the others told me that he scampered up the hills of Peleliu ahead of everyone else.

The lobby at the West Plaza Malakal had open computers for checking your e-mail. One was devoted to Japanese and the other two were in English. Lisa, the night clerk, helped us to log in to our Hotmail and other accounts. After dinner, I cleared some e-mail spam and responded to a few personal messages, including one from my brother Jim mentioning that Gabe Ineichen had called to say he was sending a CD-ROM filled with 118 good scans of 1944 Peleliu photos from an album kept by his uncle, a Navy CB. It was the same one he had sent to Pilkington. Gabe also placed an ad in the 1st Marine Division publication "Old Breed" offering the digital photos to veterans.

Tangie suggested I change my schedule and go down to Peleliu with him by boat on Friday. We would go on a speedboat coming up from the Storyboard Resort on Peleliu to Malakal. Godwin, who owns the Storyboard and Peleliu Divers, was picking up some supplies and two Japanese scuba divers at Neco Marine near our hotel. His boat was much faster than the public vessel and I could streamline my gear for the trip, leaving most of it at the hotel in Malakal. This meant forsaking the Friday dive plans and the Ngemelis drop-off, but those logistics seemed like a stretch anyway, and Tangie said he would give me the royal treatment by dedicating his weekend to guiding my exploration on Peleliu. As it turned out, he never left my side, sleeping on a futon bedroll in my cottage at the Storyboard Resort and taking me to every important site on the island.

Tangie thought that it would be best if we flew back on Sunday because we could fly over the Umurbrogol and the Rock Islands by daylight.

It is not easy to book a flight on Belau Air. Another guest at the hotel named Chris, a retired policeman from Sacramento, stayed in the room next to mine and told me that he tried and couldn't get in touch with Belau Air at all. He said their phone was disconnected and the office was always closed. Tangie must have friends in high places because all I had to do was leave it to him and he made all the arrangements. The plane would meet us on Sunday and the travel itinerary was set. All that remained was to inform Russelle at Sam's Tours of the change in plans and re-schedule the Friday diving for the following week. Thursday's dive was still on, and I would do three dives, two by day and one at night. Blue Corner was beckoning and I was looking forward to it like a child waits for Christmas morning. I knew it was within sight of Peleliu. It would be my first chance to glimpse the island that held such an important place in my mind and my father's World War II combat experience.

Tangie suggested that Dad's dog tag should go into the Peleliu Museum on the island. He said he'd mount it on a storyboard and asked me to engrave a dedication when I got back to the States. I had been worried that if I left the tag in the Umurbrogol, someone might uncover it and try to contact the family. He also wanted me to send a plaque when I returned to the States and he'd mount it on Hill 260.

My father would be fine with the donation of his dog tag to the Peleliu war museum, a former blockhouse and headquarters building scarred with damage from grenades, naval artillery and machine gun fire. He is a modest man of quiet strength and eloquence, proud to be a Marine but reticent about his own contributions, always respectful of those who served and his fellow Marine casualties of the battle. Although he was amenable to placing his dog tag in the museum on Peleliu, he frowned on the idea of a plaque that would single him out by commemorating his personal actions. My father exhibits the true principles of the Marine "Esprit de Corps." He had an exemplary civilian career as an inventive engineer and was an extraordinary father, yet the adage was true, "Once a Marine, always a Marine." Semper Fi.

The rain ceased overnight with clearing skies and the wind diminished at daybreak. I caught the early van from the West Plaza to Sam's and had a light breakfast. The dive board listed me on the boat *Tigershark* with Scott as the divemaster. Scott fetched the oxygen analyzer and I took readings and labeled my two tanks before placing them with my gear aboard the vessel. The percentage of oxygen in the Nitrox blend was very close to EANx 32, giving me a maximum overall depth of somewhere between 111 and 114 feet. Although our two dives would be on a steep wall, I knew the best sights would be at less than 100 feet.

The first dive was Ngedebus, an island whose name is often spelled in different ways. Most dive books and maps spell it with the "d," but the First Marine Division Presidential Unit Citation spells it "Ngesebus." It is just across the channel from Ngemelis. The "n" is not pronounced at all, so you call them "GED-eh-bus" and "GEM-eh-lees" respectively.

Scott gave us instructions. "Keep the wall on the left, drift with the current until you reach 750 psi, then do your safety stop and surface, inflate your safety sausage (a signaling device) and wait for the boat driver to see you." He was concerned with a couple of novice divers. Joe, the District Attorney for Yap, was my dive buddy that day. The sea creatures seemed to travel in pairs as we saw two gorgeous eagle rays; two stingrays; two whitetip sharks; four turtles, a Napoleon wrasse–a very large fish with a bump on its head very similar to the hump-headed parrotfish; and two leopard sharks (*Triakis semifasciata*) with small dark spots on their narrow bodies and ridges running from head to tail topped by a long, low fin. These are often called zebra sharks (*Stegostoma fasciatum*) since most leopards have wider splotches, but in the far Pacific you will hear both species referred to as leopards.

Sharks play an important role in Palauan culture. The iconography of designs on storyboards, the craft of carving depictions of folk tales and legends on wooden boards, reflects the images painted on beams inside the traditional Palauan village assembly hall called a *bai*. Clan ceremonies include dances about sharks and are closely linked with traditional stories handed down from one generation to the next. One rite of passage involved the taking of a shark to achieve manhood. Fishermen deal with sharks every day, and the sea has always been the domain of men in Palauan society while the women tended the land crops of taro and cassava.

Divers go to Palau for the thrill of getting up close to schools of sharks. Sadly, others use long-line fishing techniques to endanger the ecosystem through the destructive practice known as "shark finning." I would learn more about that later when I returned to Malakal. It explained why most sharks were gray, blacktip or whitetip, and it was rare to see a tiger or hammerhead.

It was my first dive in Palau. Joe and I were leading the others just ahead of the photographers and diving couples holding hands in the deep blue sea. Our actual maximum depth was 92 feet, but the equivalent enriched air depth was 71.9 feet, extending my no-decompression limit. Joe became fascinated with the behavior of the leopard sharks while I enjoyed the exotic species of striped angelfish, triggerfish, fusiliers, big-jawed wrasses, anemones and the ubiquitous butterflyfish, basslets and dartfish. We spotted a cuttlefish going through its color metamorphosis. There were numerous gobies, blennies angelfish and other species under the waters of Chuuk Lagoon and Yap, but Palau's waters were unsurpassed for plentiful aquatic life.

I caught my first glimpse of Peleliu on the dive boat at Ngedebus. The tropical island looked peaceful with gentle peaks covered in green; a silhouette that belied its fearsome threat concealed among the coral beaches, jagged hills and hidden caves sixty years ago. It seemed to float gracefully on a tranquil, multi-hued sea. The sunlight danced on the verdant terrain that was so close and yet so far away, glinting, beckoning as our boat bobbed in the gentle swells. My mind raced to catch up with its sensory impression.

My father carried the *Complete Works of Shakespeare* across the Pacific with him during World War II and kept a handwritten list of his deployments inside the cover. Shakespeare echoed in my head when he told me I would hear voices on Peleliu, "Be not afraid: the isle is full of noises" (*The Tempest*, III, I, 146). The island that I saw from the boat off Ngedebus was not the same one described in the books and memoirs of the veterans who fought there. Yet I knew the ghosts of battle looked out on the sea, for its shores had turned black with smoke and red with the blood of too many men.

The Rock Islands are like nowhere else on earth. The dangerous peaks of the Umurbrogol looked benign, blanketed under a canopy of jungle brush, framed by a light blue sky, with rays of sunlight dancing across the azure and turquoise waters through white puffy fair-weather cumulus clouds. My fellow divers scurried about the deck, satisfying their thirst and snacking on orange slices in gleeful anticipation of our next splash at Blue Corner. I was momentarily lost in the solemn beauty of an island paradise with the somber remembrance of the violence that took place and the tales of war I had read and heard.

Back at the dive shop I had telephone messages from Mayumi at the Storyboard Resort telling me that her husband Godwin would pick me up at 9:00 A.M. at Neco Marine, just down the street from the West Plaza Malakal. Tangie had also called Sam's and it was confirmed; we were headed to Peleliu on Friday morning by speedboat and flying back on Sunday night. I would have the opportunity at last to visit and photograph the battle sites. I made a mental note to review my list of what to bring and prepare for the trip.

It would have been useless to sit in the hotel that evening, and I decided to go on a night dive, momentarily bringing me back to the reality of here and now. We went to Paradise Corner, a shallow dive but with some interesting creatures including a lionfish and large Napoleon wrasse. Jonathan, Maggie's husband, was our divemaster. I remembered Steve's maxim on Yap, "There are no bad dives, there are only bad divers," and it was an apt description of the night dive. There was one barelegged diver who kicked like an eggbeater and constantly flailed his hands and arms for stability. He never left the divemaster's shoulder.

Another problem with night diving occurs when the guide points something out and everyone clusters with their lights and

66

cameras at the same spot, like paparazzi surrounding the red carpet on Oscar night. Most divers had electric light sticks, and I kept an eye on my dive buddy Mike with his identifiable green chemical glow stick.

Back on the boat after the dive, Mike said, "What were you using for a dive light? It was the brightest one I've ever seen." I told him about the iodized gas HID technology and he asked, "Why did you turn it off?" I responded that I got tired of the crowd and the crazy diver floundering helplessly like a hooked mackerel and had intentionally turned my light off. Floating in the black void and watching the spectacle was a much better alternative. Mike called me the "stealth diver."

Blue Corner 6

The Republic of Palau is an archipelago with over 70 islands. It is a rippling ribbon of coral that extends from the northeast to the southwest approximately 600 miles from the Philippines. The coral formations, starkly eroded limestone islands and the convergence of the Pacific Ocean and the Philippine Sea provide the ingredients for unsurpassed scuba diving. The islands' terrain runs the gamut geologically from sandy beaches and dense foliage to rugged limestone cliffs with impassable jungle.

The Rock Islands of Palau arguably contain the best sites for scuba divers on the planet. Their names are legendary: Blue Corner, Blue Holes, Peleliu Express, Ngedebus, Ulong, Shark City, and Saies Drop-Off. They are world-class dives with changing, high-velocity currents and abundant aquatic life.

The best of them all is Blue Corner, a sensational wall dive. Imagine two elbows of coral with a shelf in between. The Blue Holes to the north are spectacular dives by themselves. You get there by boat through the German Channel, literally a ditch or canal cut through the hard coral easily recognized from the air and clearly marked in the water. You can see Peleliu toward the southwest when you get to the end of the channel as you travel by boat from Koror or Malakal.

The day was clearing with blue sky and sunshine. Divers approach the corner's shelf-like promontory from the north or the south, depending upon the current. On this day we approached from the southeast. We determined the direction by looking at the gorgonia—sea fans (*Melitea squarata*) and whip corals (*Ellisellidae*) from the surface. You must be constantly aware because the current may change at any time during the dive, and it did on this visit. The dive began like many others, but eventually and inevitably I found myself in the midst of a tremendously exciting dynamic of electrifying underwater energy that rose to a crescendo of action at Blue Corner increasing with the velocity of the current. The visibility was easily 100 to 200 feet.

Most of us would have been satisfied with the gorgonians and fishes on the wall leading up to Blue Corner. There were many species: bluefin and yellowtail tuna, damselfish, huge anemones, black stripe or bar jack, goatfish, gobies, chevron barracuda, clown triggerfish (*Balistoides conspicillum*), big-eyed jacks and lots of sharks. A large and ferociously territorial triggerfish with human-like teeth protected its nest. The divemaster wrote "Danger" on his slate. The fish and sharks seemed suspended in the fast-moving water while we watched. The sharks swim freely with, across and against the strong current. Scuba divers are able to hold on, but must remain close to the reef or risk being swept up to the surface prematurely.

We saw a large Napoleon wrasse, a hump-headed parrotfish, and abundant schools of gray reef (*Carcharhinus amblyrhyncos*), whitetip, blacktip and widebody silvertip sharks like the ones we saw in Chuuk. Sea bream, blue chromis, big-eye trevally (*Caranx sexfasciatus*) and that large triggerfish protecting its nest made our dive unique. Later, I discovered that Blue Corner is an exceptional dive and different each time you plunge underwater.

I could feel the tension build as adrenalin rushed through my veins. That's when I took out my reef hook, fastened the large metal hook to a rock, tethered myself by letting out four or five feet of line and enjoyed the pelagic parade. The reef hook is a large fishhook without the sharp barb tied to four to six feet of nylon line. At the other end is a 4" piece of PVC pipe, 1" in diameter, used as a handgrip to give the diver an option to hold on to it as a handle or attach it to a D-ring or caribiner on the BC jacket. According to Eric Hanauer, a dive guide at Sam's Tours invented the reef hook.[1]

The shoaling fishes held fast against the strong current; the fusiliers maintained their position and I wished that I didn't have to let go. Then, regretfully, I had to end my dive, drift to the surface and inflate my safety sausage as a floating signal for the boat to

70

come pick me up.

Novice divers should note that many guidebooks suggest you must be an expert to attempt Blue Corner. Although the current can take you to the Philippines, and six divers were stranded and eventually died off Palau following a failed dive trip in February 1994, if you stick with your group and keep an eye on your dive guide you will be fine. The best advice you can follow is to make sure your gear is in proper order; find your point of neutral buoyancy with proper weighting, prepare your reef hook line for deployment before the dive, make a gradual descent, and enjoy the experience. Sometimes you may find Blue Corner with a minimal current, but you'll always see a lot of marine life. After one or two dives, you too will come under the spell of Blue Corner.

Chevron Barracuda. (Credit: Photo by Jack Connick. Copyright 2003, Jack Connick Creative Services, Inc.)

One of the disturbing things that I saw on the docks next o Sam's earlier was a result of the booming Taiwanese tourist ndustry. The Chinese come to Palau on bargain-priced package ours for vacation, fishing and snorkeling. This is all well and good, but one of the divemasters told me that the Taiwanese fishing boats had been fined heavily in Palau for long-line shark-fin fishing; literally cutting the dorsal and tail fins from sharks and throwing the carcasses overboard. I had wondered why there was a lack of variety in the species we saw. Nearly every time Palauan customs inspectors looked into the holds of these trawlers, there were countless shark fins. The boats dry the fins out at sea and then store them in ice for shipping. Eventually, they find their way into costly delicacies such as shark-fin soup. The fishing boats outnumber the customs boats by a wide margin. I expressed my dismay to Sam as we looked at the rusted vessels next to his dock used for the Taiwanese long-line fishing trips. I made a note to contact Bill Raynor of The Nature Conservancy when I got back to the United States.

Footnotes
[1] Eric Hanauer, *Diving Micronesia*, Locust Valley, New York: Aqua Quest Publications, 2001, p. 71.

chapter

7

"The Jungle Does Grow"
~Everett P. Pope, April 2004

Neco Marine is very close to the West Plaza Malakal, just past the oil storage tanks, pipes and valves; a familiar sight in the islands near the sea. Mobil or Shell Oil facilities lined the roads in Chuuk, Yap and Malakal. Tangie and I prepared to meet Godwin's Storyboard/Peleliu Divers boat at Neco's dock. Their complex, specializing in Yamaha sales and service, scuba courses, and excursions, has a large swimming pool for diver training. It was in a clean, modern building and the pool deck was spotless. The store and showroom were air-conditioned and the staff was friendly.

The road to Neco Marine led past the Mini Mart and its concrete parking lot stained with betel nut juice. I carried my gear in a backpack and a briefcase with a shoulder strap. The air was heavy with humidity and at 9:00 A.M. the sun was bright in the sky. I wore blue jeans; a lightweight ventilated SPF-15 shirt, and National Geographic waterproof hiking shoes.

Godwin arrived early in his boat from Peleliu to load supplies. He is Peleliuan and his wife Mayumi is Japanese. They run the Storyboard Resort together. Mayumi takes care of the guests including the lodging, food and gift shop, while Godwin owns and operates an outstanding dive operation on Peleliu. He is an expert divemaster who is justifiably proud of his safety record with all levels of scuba divers in dangerous currents on deep reefs. Everyone I met praised his diving skill and underwater leadership. In addition, he has an outgoing personality and I enjoyed speaking with him about diving. He was curious about Nitrox; I wouldn't be surprised if Peleliu Divers eventually blends Nitrox mixes for its divers. The depths around the island may limit the possibilities for

Nitrox diving due to EANx32's maximum of 111 feet, presenting the danger of oxygen toxicity if you go deeper. An alternative is to blend a custom mix with 28% O2, permitting a maximum depth of 132 fsw, but it would require a significant investment in equipment. Godwin takes care of his guests and runs thrilling and safe diving excursions for Japanese and American divers or anyone else who has a passion for the sport and wants to experience the best reef diving in the world.

Godwin asked the Yamaha service technician at Neco Marine to take a look at one of his twin 200-HP Yamaha outboards because it was making a grinding sound. The mechanic said it was fine for the time being, and Godwin remarked that he'd need to find a replacement part soon. The Yap dive boats featured twin 100s, and Sam's Tours' boats on Palau were outfitted with 115s and 140s. Yamaha manufactured virtually all of the motors.

Tangie and I chatted with the staff at Neco in cool comfort while Godwin signed for the food and equipment and loaded it on his boat. Everything was ready in the blink of an eye. Godwin was anxious to get back to Peleliu where divers eagerly waited for him to take them out to the reefs and walls of Peleliu Corner and Peleliu Express. There were only two other passengers on the boat with us (both Japanese divers) as we pulled away from the dock.

Most dive operators take the German Channel out to the dive sites, but Godwin knew a route away from all the boat traffic. He was an expert skipper and headed northeast out of the harbor, motoring slowly until we cleared Malakal and left behind the radio towers on the quarry hill overlooking the harbor. Then he revved the engines and accelerated swiftly through the sparkling waters and narrow shoals of the Rock Islands.

There are two main water transports to Peleliu if you don't own or charter your own vessel: the public boat that takes about two hours, or the Storyboard Resort's speedboat with Godwin behind the wheel. His customized craft ripped through unmarked channels as if he was unconcerned about the possibly faulty bearing in the port outboard. Godwin's boat seemed to fly through the unfathomable beauty of Palau's Rock Islands; sometimes coming so close I felt like I could reach out and touch the limestone. We raced past gravity-defying archways; caves at the waterline, hidden beaches, and geological features that made the islands appear as if they

Rock Islands on boat to Peleliu from Malakal (above and below).

were perched on a precarious pedestal like a mushroom cap. A few of the islands looked like they might collapse on themselves when the sea finally eroded their foundations. The water was so clear that I could see the sand on the bottom with dangerous rocks under the surface. Godwin relied on his own memory and the expert knowledge of a man who lives for the sea as he masterfully guided the speeding boat through narrow openings lacking channel markers or buoys in waters with a mosaic of turquoise, blue and green colors. We reached Peleliu by following a southwest route.

The sound of the outboards made too much noise for conversation, and I joined the Japanese divers in shooting digital video footage while bouncing through the amazing spectacle around us. Godwin knew the way by heart.

As we got closer to Peleliu, Tangie pointed out Carp Island, an exclusive Japanese resort with sandy beaches near the popular southwest dive sites. It usually takes the Koror and Malakal dive operators up to an hour to reach the southwest sites, but divers from Carp Island and Peleliu can get there in just minutes earlier in the day before the other boats arrive. Carp Island was just north of Peleliu and we could see our destination looming in the distance as we passed the Ngedcbus and Blue Corner sites I dived the previous day.

Godwin slowed the boat as we motored through the rocky shallows on the northwest side of the island. We saw a few residential and commercial buildings as we approached the dock including a clean and well-maintained green structure open on the first level in the Key West style. A sign on the landing proclaimed, "Welcome to Peleliu State Land of Enchantment."

There was a boat tied to the dock with lettering indicating it belonged to the Peleliu Marine Enforcement Division. Six or seven Japanese divers were waiting for us on the landing with their scuba tanks, gear bags and coolers with beverages and lunch. It was low tide and we had to step up to the concrete dock. We threw our baggage in the back of a pickup truck as Godwin's crew loaded the scuba tanks on the boat for its next trip out to the reefs. Tangie and I rode with Godwin while the truck delivered our luggage to the Storyboard Resort. The truck was missing a door handle, but we were on our way in short order for the brief ride to the Storyboard.

At last, after many e-mails and telephone calls, I met Mayumi. She showed me to cottage #3, nestled in the coconut palms at the end of a shaded sandy path lined with limestone walls. The cabin was elevated with stairs leading to a landing where we removed our shoes before entering. There were slippers in the cottage for us to wear while inside to keep the sand off the floor. The floor consisted of wide wooden planks with large gaps in between. As I changed from denims into cargo shorts, coins fell out of my pocket and rolled around the floor before inevitably slipping through the cracks down into the sand below.

Tangie insisted that he would be my private battlefield guide, translator, transportation coordinator, driver and steadfast companion. Tangie was the most dedicated guide I could have imagined as he cancelled other requests from American and Japanese groups and decided to accompany me without any other travelers to Peleliu. Mayumi arranged to have a futon delivered for Tangie. The futon was similar to a thin mattress that rolled up easily, quite unlike the couches and elaborate furniture known as futons in the United States. Tangie was content to sleep on the futon mat placed on the floor in the corner of my room closest to the veranda. The room was large enough for a double bed; a nightstand; wide window sills where Tangie placed the citation portfolio that Everett Pope had given him; a closet; shelves; and a bathroom with sink, countertop, shower, and toilet. There was hot water in the shower. The handle for the toilet's flushing mechanism was broken, so I had to grab a string attached through the hole on the side and pull it. It worked perfectly once I figured it out. Although the room was not air-conditioned, a ceiling fan circulated the air and there were electrical outlets to charge my iPAQ Pocket PC, cell phone and digital video camera.

Tangie suggested that I rent a van and he would drive it. I agreed to the deal and Tangie disappeared to get the vehicle. While I waited for him to return and drive us to the landing beaches for our first afternoon on Peleliu, I went out to the private beach at the Storyboard. The Philippine Sea was only a few feet from the veranda and I walked down the path to the shore. Looking across the water, I could see Ngedebus and Blue Corner beyond the waves breaking on the fringing reef at low tide about 400 yards from shore. It was pleasant to relax on a hammock for a few minutes of peace and contemplation before catching up with the jottings in my journal. This was a tranquil spot, yet I felt as if there were eyes in the bushes and I sensed that the ghosts of the past were all around us in the jungle, hills, beaches, bunkers, tunnels and caves. I knew I would have many moments of silent reflection like this during my stay, remembering those valiant souls who came face-to-face with their own mortality on the killing grounds of Peleliu.

The journey through the Rock Islands took us past the exciting reefs and walls that were the stuff of scuba divers' dreams. How could I imagine what the Marines were thinking as they made their way through the reefs in a perilous beach assault? My father had told me about his pre-invasion beach reconnaissance swim as a Marine "volunteer" with the Navy's UDT-6. How could my own scuba diving with state-of-the-art 21st century scuba gear even pretend to approximate my father's swimming for hours in the shallow reefs off Peleliu's Orange Beach? His recollection was clear and specific:

> The Navy destroyers and battleships shelled the island while we were in the water. You could see the vortex of the shell in the air as the water rippled from the shock wave. After our mission, we waited in the water until they could get in close enough to pick us up. During beachhead demolitions we found many 2-horned anti-ship mines laced to horned scullies and coral cairns. They were 100 lb. Type 98, set out about 100 yards from the beach. Some of them were not armed, the safety pin wasn't pulled, and they were not there the day before. Amazingly, they had also buried some aircraft bombs in the beach with pressure fuses. We also found fuel drums laced to the fringing coral. The Japanese swimmers had to work like hell to get that done so quickly.[1]

Mayumi made our lunches and I did my best to eat the ham, cheese and lettuce sandwich but I had the strange feeling the ham was actually Spam. Iced tea helped to wash it down, along with two Micronesia-style bananas identical to the ones on the *Truk Odyssey*; stubby versions of the Chiquitas we have in the States. The quiet solitude in the beach hammock on the northwest corner of Peleliu was broken only by the sound of a rooster crowing, a foreshadowing of the feral chickens we would see crossing the roads. I had never seen a chicken on a leash in my life until Peleliu, where they are tethered to keep them from running wild

Just for fun, I took a GPS reading outside the cottage, our base of operations for this journey on Peleliu. It was exactly 8,679 miles to my home in Temple Terrace, Florida and the GPS coordinates were: N 07° 02.318 and E 134° 15.179.

I asked Mayumi if she would open her gift shop. She smiled and graciously obliged although the phone was ringing off the hook and she was busy folding T-shirts while keeping an eye on her young son playing nearby. I purchased a few souvenirs: T-shirts for my father and sisters, a wall hanging for my mother, and for myself a key chain and a couple of "Peleliu Divers" T-shirts. I took another brief respite in the hammock where Tangie had eaten his own meatless lunch before fetching the vehicle.

Tangie returned with a Toyota minivan. The driver's seat was on the right, and the cost seemed steep since the exterior driver's side rear-view mirror was missing, the dashboard was coming apart at the seams from the heat, the windshield was cracked, the door handles and locks were in disrepair, and the button to control the sunroof dangled on a wire from the switch plate above. But the motor worked, the wheels turned, and its bumper sticker said "Marines." It was fine with me because I stood on the back seat and shot video through the roof as Tangie drove to the beaches and airfield.

My landside exploration of this quiet island began with a drive through downtown Peleliu where the 600 residents live. Tangie stopped at the Governor's office for a visit. Everyone knew him. The road was wide with reflective yellow lane markers. There was a terrestrial microwave tower for telephone service. Many homes lined the roadway with cars and trucks in driveways. There were churches and a few stores. At the Peleliu Elementary School, a fence surrounded the athletic field and school buses were parked next to the building.

We drove in a loop around the north end of the island near Amber Beach before returning to downtown and then down the East Road toward the swamplands. Tangie pointed out Radar Hill on the left. The Marines had taken the hill in late September 1944, but the Japanese remained hidden in caves, conforming to their defense system plan. Despite reaching the summit, dangerous enemy lurked below embedded in limestone crevices. When the 323rd Army Division attacked the hill in October, there was such ferocious fighting that they believed they were the first to assault that area. The strength of the hidden resistance undoubtedly contributed to the misperception. This was a battlefield where soldiers could take the peak of a hill and not control the entire ridge because it was like a termite mound teeming with lethal pests hiding underground.

Radar Hill. (Photo © 2004 Patrick Finelli)

Major Gayle's 2nd Battalion, 5th Marines was also involved in the advance on the highland region. Reduction of the cave systems was tried with tanks, a 75-mm gun, bazookas, and flamethrowers, but all they succeeded in doing was to help the forces reach the summit while large numbers of Japanese remained in the caves further down the slopes.

Harry Gailey's book underscores the work of the demolition teams in eliminating an enemy that would rather die than surrender, "Some of the caves were so inaccessible and well-protected that only the nearly superhuman efforts of the demolition men succeeded in sealing their entrances."[2] Radar Hill was on the causeway across from a pond where locals farmed milkfish. Next to the pond, protected by a chain link fence, we could see the rusted barrel of a five-inch Japanese gun.

Tangie casually remarked that there were saltwater crocodiles in the swamp near the milkfish pond. I had seen pictures of crocodiles in the open water and knew they were plentiful on Anguar and Australia, but hadn't realized they lived on Peleliu as well.

On our way to the southwest end of the island, we visited the Peleliu Museum. It was a former blockhouse and headquarters. The building is pockmarked with major bomb damage from battleship artillery and hits from rifle, machine gun (MG), and bazooka rounds. This was the blockhouse that Chesty Puller vehemently complained to the Navy about because it was not touched by Naval gunfire (NGF) on or before D-Day. There is glass over the damage preserving the destruction, a reminder of war's unrelenting violence, unlike most museums that contain military memorabilia.

The museum was filled with relics and mementos donated by veterans and their descendants. We walked slowly through the displays of rifles, machine guns, bazooka tubes, ammunition boxes, bullets, mortars, grenades, torpedoes, helmets, mess kits, uniforms, gas masks, footwear, bottles, kettles, swords, belts, fuses, torn flags, and Colonel Nakagawa's telephone.

Tangie asked me to pose for a video while holding Nakagawa's phone to my ear. Sweat poured from my brow. Then he picked up a Japanese helmet with two machine gun holes that had perforated the metal. This was not a military surplus curiosity shop, but a somber memorial revealing the tragedy of war. There is an American section and a Japanese section in the museum. There is a corridor lined with books and letters written by veterans and many maps and pictures, both personal and historical. There are several photographs of the airfield; individual platoons and squads, Major General W.H. Rupertus and Colonel "Chesty" Puller, the dedication of the cemetery, and many emblems of the 1st Marine Division.

Peleliu Museum (former blockhouse and HQ building).
(Photo © 2004 Patrick Finelli)

Tangie suggested that I leave my father's aluminum dog tag with him and he would place it in the museum. I sent him an engraved stainless steel plate (2 1/4" high and 4 1/2" wide) when I got back home along with matching screws for mounting on a custom storyboard for display with the dog tag. The inscription reads:

82

Sgt. Patrick L. Finelli
USMC

UDT-6 Orange Beach Recon
3/1 and 2/7, Umurbrogol Mtn, Hill 260
Wounded by bayonet, Sept. 26, 1944
The Battle of Peleliu

Placed in tribute by his son, Patrick M. Finelli, Ph.D.
March 20, 2004

Although I had seen Peleliu earlier in the week while diving
Ngedebus Wall and the Blue Corner, nothing prepared me for the
shock of the topographic and geologic formations, the sheer and
treacherous limestone cliffs in the Umurbrogol, rugged hills littered
with caves and tunnels, the hard corals of the White Beaches and
The Point, and the fringing reef thousands of yards beyond the
wide sand of the Orange Beaches.

Sherman tank treads at White Beach 1. (Photo © 2004 Patrick Finelli)
GPS: N 07° 00.358', E 134° 13.364'

83

We arrived at White Beach 1 at low tide. As Tangie walked ahead, I noticed Sherman tank treads in a tidal pool. We had seen a pillbox driving down the West Road to the beach. During the invasion, the tracked LVTs[3] were able to climb over the fringing reef onto the shelf to approach the shore, but mortar fire knocked out more than a dozen. Many of the LCMs[4], capable of carrying a squad, platoon, vehicles or a 30-ton tank, had to stop at the edge of the reef where the assault troops disembarked under intense fire. Then they had to make their way to the beach until the Seabees (CB) made pontoons of multiple steel cells, two or more wide, and of varying lengths. The pontoons were carried on the sides of the LSTs[5] and then dropped and motored over the shallow reefs to be put in position. They also used them as barges with mobile cranes and/or large outboard motors. Pontoons at Peleliu were used as causeways for tanks and other vehicles to reach the shore. Many pontoons were still in place as part of the boat basin at the south end of Orange Beach.

The Point was to the north as we looked west across the reef. The defensive pillboxes, foxholes and gun emplacements were still there. Captain George P. Hunt and his "K" Company, 3rd Battalion, 1st Marines must have drawn the toughest invasion assignment. White Beach had to have been the most difficult place to land. It is entirely formed by hard coral with nowhere to dig in for protection. To the north, or left side as the troops landed on the beach, a promontory "Point" extends into the sea with heavily fortified concrete and limestone pillboxes, backed by foxholes and spider holes carved out of hard limestone and coral. Hunt's men faced camouflaged anti-boat guns and six 25mm heavy machine guns targeting the landing beach from this location. I went into the pillbox and took a picture looking out at the view seen by the Japanese gunners. The bunkers with machine guns backed by mortars in foxholes had an unobstructed target field to cover the beach with enfilading fire.

The pictures below show the landing beaches with a wide expanse between the fringing reef and the shore. The water on the reef is shallow even at high tide. The Marines were pinned down in a fusillade under impossible conditions, caught in the crossfire in 115° F equatorial sun against Japanese counter-attacks and mortars launched from an anti-tank ditch. Snipers waited in spider holes on the beach.

Hunt and his men of "K" Company pressed on through force of will against virtually impregnable defenses. It was not a "walk over" by any means; it was rough and the outcome of this battle of attrition hinged in the balance. The courage of those troops, asked to do the impossible against long odds, is nearly incomprehensible. The beaches, corals and rocky shores were dangerous for us on a spring day in 2004. It is unimaginable to conceive of what it was like in September 1944. Tangie and I found spent shells and bullets wherever we looked.

White Beach 1 and The Point, looking NW. (Photo © 2004 Patrick Finelli)
GPS: N 07° 00.385, E 134° 13.332

Command intelligence held the prevailing view that naval bombardment and air assault could soften resistance, but the enemy entrenched in caves and bunkers withstood the shelling. It was emotionally overwhelming to read the plaque Tangie had placed in September 1999 dedicated to Captain George Hunt, a remembrance of the tremendous sacrifice made by the 26-year old company commander and the Marines under his command.

The order of battle assigned Captain Hunt's company to the extreme left flank closest to The Point at White Beach 1. An LST transported the company's amtracs to an offshore point of departure well off the reef. The LVTs formed assault waves after driving off the bow ramp of the LSTs. The fringing reef made it impossible for many landing craft, except the tracked vehicles. The image below shows the Marine amtracs heading for the beach. The Point is at the top of the photograph, with White and then the Orange Beaches just above another fortified promontory.

Amphibious assault, D-Day, 15 September 1944.
(Courtesy of Marine Historical Division)

Marines wading ashore.(Photo Courtesy Gabe Ineichen)

Field of fire from the pillbox at The Point, looking south.
(Photo © 2004 Patrick Finelli)

Pillbox at White Beach 2. (Photo © 2004 Patrick Finelli)
GPS: N 07° 00.052, E 134° 13.312

Beach landing, 1944. (Photo Courtesy Gabe Ineichen)

D-Day +2, 1944. (Photo Courtesy Gabe Ineichen)

Marines take cover in tank traps. (Photo Courtesy Gabe Ineichen)

Orange Beach is sandy, but the Marines would have to cross at least 200 yards of shallow coral from the breakwater to take cover in tank traps or dig their own foxholes. Many found protection behind LVTs that made it to shore.

Tangie paused to scoop some sand from Orange Beach into an empty water bottle. With each handful, I thought of my father swimming with UDT Team 6 to clear the obstacles while artillery shells pounded the shore. The reef looked exactly as he described it with a breakwater hundreds of yards from the shore and shallow water from the fringing reef to the sandy beach.

The Underwater Demolition Teams (UDTs) were a relatively new concept, fulfilling an important need in amphibious warfare. The lack of beach reconnaissance and underwater demolition of obstacles contributed to the high number of Marine casualties at Tarawa on November 20, 1943. Commanders needed a force to clear the beaches and provide information about the depth of the water, currents and surge, rocks and corals, the consistency and slope of the sand, and tidal patterns in addition to observing the enemy's beach defenses.

The UDT units were established on May 7, 1943 and their first combat deployment was in the Marshall Islands. Commander Francis D. Fane's book, *Naked Warriors*, recounted the history of the elite underwater demolitions teams that preceded the special forces trained for unconventional warfare, the Navy SEALs. SEAL is an acronym for Sea, Air and Land. The SEAL units were established during the Vietnam War in 1962 under the administration of President John F. Kennedy.

My father corresponded with Fane. The author and historian wrote a letter granting rights to Dad to carve a model of the UDT swimmer based upon a photograph Fane had taken and reproduced in his book. Fane's letter says the photograph was, "Among the first photos taken underwater with a hand-held camera."[6] It depicts a UDT member reaching out to an obstacle covered with barbed wire and spikes while holding a Hagensen pack of C-3 explosives. The swimmer wears only fins, mask and swim trunks.

90

Sketch of "Naked Warrior" by P.L. Finelli

UDT teams in the Pacific were deployed at Eniwetok, Saipan, Guam, Tinian, Anguar, Ulithi, Peleliu, the Philippines, Iwo Jima and Okinawa. The underwater demolition teams on Peleliu began clearing obstacles on September 12, three days before the invasion. Admiral Oldendorf proclaimed they were "the most formidable which we encountered in the entire Pacific."[7]

Regarding Peleliu, Fane wrote, "At the same time I was First Lieutenant and Cargo Officer on board the USN ammunition ship *U.S.S. Mauna Loa* unloading in Kossol Passage within sight of Marines fighting inland of the beach."[8]

My father provided his own recollection of the UDTs:

> We were told that there was a screw-up at Tinian involving the Marine Recons under Capt. Jim Jones and the UDTs under someone named Kauffman.[9] The UDTs didn't get to the beach and the Marine Recons did. It also involved a dispute over "high water" responsibility. General Holland Smith, revered in the Corps as the Patron of Amphibious Landings, felt that his Marines, in particular the Recons, could and should do the whole job of Recon and Clearing. The problem was Recon was small and needed elsewhere.
>
> General Smith was very upset with the Navy and the Army and sent out search teams to find Demolition men who could be spared for UDT work in concert with his beloved Recon group. My guess is that those of us in aviation were expendable so Captain Sweet volunteered us. He volunteered himself, me and another Marine for a special assignment. I was a good swimmer, trained in bomb disposal and demolitions. We were dispatched to Eniwetok where we were given physicals and swim tests. OSS personnel indoctrinated us with rigorous training in the use of a swim mask and fins. Captain Sweet never participated, he just observed and took notes. At the conclusion of training, we broke up and went different ways. My group was assigned to the U. S. S. Clemson, APD-31, a converted World War I vessel. Two destroyers in our fleet, the Noa and the Fullem, hit each other and one of them went to the bottom with the explosives from the ABLE[10] unit. After OSS's loss, UDT Team 6 took over and the fleet kept going. Swim teams were matched for reconnaissance on Peleliu.
>
> Our job was recon on enemy held beaches in September 1944. The Navy destroyers and battleships shelled the island while we were in the water. You could see the vortex of the shell in the air as the water rippled from the shock wave. After our mission, we waited in the water until they could get in close enough to pick us up.[11]

As we walked from Orange Beach to the van, we paused at the cemetery where we saw the remnants of the 1st Marine Division's chapel and two obelisks built by the U. S. Army. The bodies had been moved to Arlington National Cemetery, and flowers spelled out "USA" between the monuments. Tangie pointed out the flower of a plant he called "Moses in a boat" and I realized that there were a number of them growing in my backyard in Florida.

Our next destination was the airfield. After months of correspondence with Rob Amaral prior to my journey, I couldn't help but imagine his uncle, Sgt. Edward A. Amaral, Squad Leader of Marine Assault Rifle Company "B," 1st Battalion, 5th Marines, a veteran of Peleliu and later Okinawa, walking across the airfield standing upright against hostile fire. Rob was proud to be his godson and nephew. He respects and honors his Uncle Ed's Bronze Star and Purple Heart to this day. Rob's father, Technical Sgt. David J. Amaral served in the Army's 609th Hospital Ship Platoon, crossing the Atlantic twenty-four times. Rob thought that most of 1/5 had been wiped out. His uncle came down with dengue fever and suffered other ills after his service.

Peleliu Airfield. (Photo © 2004 Patrick Finelli)

Peleliu Airfield 1944. (Photo Courtesy Gabe Ineichen)

LVT(A)–5. (Photo © 2004 Patrick Finelli)

Tangie turned down a road on the west after driving across the airfield. It wasn't very long before we saw three amphibious vehicles: an LVT–4 that had been moved from the beach and two LVT (A)–5s, one missing its turret.

LVT(A)–5. (Photo © 2004 Patrick Finelli)

Japanese Power Plant. (Photo © 2004 Patrick Finelli)

Japanese Power Plant (left), 1944. (Photo Courtesy Gabe Ineichen)

The road led to several Japanese airport buildings, their walls overgrown with plants and vines.

Japanese Airfield Administration Building.
(Photo © 2004 Patrick Finelli)

Administration Building (center left), 1944. (Photo Courtesy Gabe Ineichen)

There were rusted hulks of Japanese light tanks similar to the ones I had seen on the *San Francisco Maru*, only these had been stopped in their tracks during a futile counter-offensive to defend the airfield. The enemy defenses had included pillboxes and sniper patrols in the woods. A blockhouse was visible from an embankment where the infantry Marines had taken up positions around LVT (A)s. The 2nd Battalion, 5th Marines were deployed along the south, with the 1st Battalion, 5th Marines to their left as they prepared to take the open airfield while waiting for the Sherman tanks to arrive. Soon, two columns of Japanese light tanks moved from protected cover into the open. Some of them had infantry strapped to the outside, sacrificially protecting the three-man crew, but not for long. The tanks were slower and lighter than the Sherman tanks. It was an armored *banzai* charge, met with punishing grenades, bazookas, automatic rifle fire, and a barrage from four Sheman tanks. There were approximately a dozen Japanese tanks, but all were destroyed in a matter of hours.

Japanese Ha-Go type 95 light tank.
(Photo © 2004 Patrick Finelli)

Captured Japanese tank, 1944. (Photo Courtesy Gabe Ineichen)

Japanese Ha-Go type 95 light tank.
(Photo © 2004 Patrick Finelli)

Japanese tank, 1944. (Photo Courtesy Gabe Ineichen)

Japanese Ha-Go Type 95 light tank.
(Photo © 2004 Patrick Finelli)

American LVT(A)–1. (Photo by Tangie Hesus)
GPS: N 07° 00.447', E 134° 14.057'

100

Opposite side of the LVT(A)–1 with 37mm gun.
(Photo © 2004 Patrick Finelli)

American amtracs, LVTs, 1944. (Photo Courtesy Gabe Ineichen)

Japanese school building. (Photo © 2004 Patrick Finelli)

The Japanese school building was the last structure on our list for the day. Tangie pointed out cassava plants with the starchy root from which tapioca is derived, betel nut palms and a taro root plantation. There were blue canvas shelters to offer protection from the sun when the women harvested the taro.

We went to the quarry through the East Road, briefly driving along the Causeway constructed over a pond and swamp by Seabees for tanks and troops. A sign pointed the way to Bloody Nose Ridge, and the Army and Marine Corps monuments. We drove up to the foothills overlooking the Horseshoe Valley to see the Medal of Honor and the First Marine Division memorials. There was a Japanese Shinto shrine nearby. From there, we saw The Umurbrogol; Five Sisters; Five Brothers; Hill 140 in the middle of the Horseshoe Valley; Hill 300, the highest point on the island; Hill 205, next to the airfield; and Pope Hill. It was a clear day with an unparalleled view that belied the horrific battles sixty years ago in these same hills and valleys.

The 200mm gun overlooking the Horseshoe and airport might have inflicted serious damage. The OP (observation post) was

200 mm artillery emplacement, 2004. (Photo © Patrick Finelli)

200 mm artillery, 1944. (Photo Courtesy Gabe Ineichen)

103

nearly invisible, although noted military photojournalist Phil Orr told me that the gun was never used. No 200mm shells were found on Peleliu.

We visited Purple Beach, now Honeymoon Beach, and then finally the Peace Park to catch the refreshing sea breeze. Tangie read a Palauan dedication as we watched the waves crashing through holes in the limestone to end a memorable afternoon

Blow holes at the Peace Park.(Photo © 2004 Patrick Finelli)

The research for my trip began when I interviewed Everett Pope, awarded the Medal of Honor for gallantry on Peleliu.[12] He had visited the island on the occasion of the 50th anniversary of the battle and told me that Micronesia, the Republic of Palau and Peleliu in particular are known primarily as premier scuba diving destinations. He reminded me that the jungle has overtaken the battle sites and the other debris of war, and that there were many large artifacts from the battle, but the terrain was virtually unrecognizable because nature and quarrying had reclaimed the rocky hills. I looked forward to climbing Pope Hill. Tangie carried Major Pope's Medal of Honor Citation and a photograph with him wherever we went.

The next morning Tangie and I headed for the hills. Our plan was to climb the ridge to Pope Hill, then cross the Horseshoe to Hill 300 and Hill 260. I brought my video camera, a snapshot camera, the Leki® trekking staff, a Swiss Army® knife, binoculars and the GPS. Pope Hill had been known as Walt's Ridge or Hill 100 until the Governor renamed it. Most of the peaks were known by their elevation, but when we got to the summit my GPS indicated the elevation was actually 183' rather than the 100' indicated by its original name. Quarrying had cut into one side of Pope Hill. The climb was steep with slippery inclines and took us through tangled brush. I worked my way up by holding onto branches, using the staff for leverage, and following Tangie's zigzag path. He carried only his backpack.

I took a snapshot of Tangie with Pope's MOH Citation Folio at the summit to send to Everett Pope when I got back to Florida. There were many rounds of ammunition and spent shells on the

Tangie Hesus climbing Pope Hill, March 20.
(Photo © 2004 Patrick Finelli)

ground in the Horseshoe Valley. Pope Hill overlooked the East
Road, the Causeway, quarry trucks and machines for mining
next to piles of gravel. It faced Hill 300 and the Five Sisters.
Tangie found an exploded mortar fuse. I found a 12.7 mm (Ho-
103) Japanese machine gun bullet. He was surprised to find a
.30-caliber American shell casing from Pope's company near the
summit.

Pope Hill looking up from quarry in the Horseshoe.
(Photo © 2004 Patrick Finelli)
GPS: N 07° 00.726', E 134° 14.274'

On the way up Pope Hill we found debris from an Avenger
spread out over the western part of the hillside near the summit.
Phil Orr told me he thought that only Corsairs flew over Peleliu,
but Tangie insisted this was an Avenger. There were two
manufacturers of the large plane. General Motors made the TBM
and Grumman produced the TBF. The fuselage was 40 feet long
and the wingspan 54 feet, making it one of the larger carrier-based
planes. It had a range of 1,000 miles and could climb to 30,000
feet. The images below show four recent photos from the Avenger
airplane wreck on Pope Hill, and one picture of a Corsair "wheels-

106

Tangie Hesus holding Everett Pope's Medal of Honor Citation and
.30-caliber American shell at summit.
(Photo © 2004 Patrick Finelli)
GPS: N 07° 00.707', E 134° 14.310', Elevation: 183'

107

Tangie Hesus holding exploded mortar fuse.
(Photos © 2004 Patrick Finelli)

down" bombing run over the Umurbrogol in 1944.

Phil, an accomplished military archaeologist, spent a couple of weeks combing the jungle for artifacts in July 2004, a few months after my visit. He confirmed the wreck was definitely an Avenger. He had determined that the engine was at the impact point, and it came apart scattering many pieces of the plane downhill from the engine on the ridge. Phil found one of the .50-caliber guns, a major find that had been on his wish list for many years.

Avenger wreckage at impact. (Photos © 2004 Patrick Finelli)

While Tangie lingered at the wreckage, I headed back down. About fifty feet from the bottom I found myself overlooking a cliff. I couldn't remember whether Tangie led us up the north or south side of it, and I carefully negotiated across the top edge looking for a good place to descend. At last I found a spot that looked promising. Grabbing onto a branch and using my staff to brace myself, I turned backward to gently reach the next level, feet first. Suddenly, the branch snapped and I tumbled about twenty feet, losing my binoculars, GPS, and sunglasses. The camera case and Swiss Army® knife were still attached to my belt. I found my

Avenger propeller and engine debris on Pope Hill. (Photos © 2004 Patrick Finelli)

Close-up of Avenger engine. (Photo © 2004 Patrick Finelli)

Wheels-down Corsair bombing run over Bloody Nose Ridge.
(PhotoCourtesy Gabe Ineichen)

lost items after a careful search under dense growth and wet leaves from storms earlier in the week. Thankfully, the only thing that broke was the belt clip for the GPS. There is no way I can possibly comprehend how the Marines survived such treacherous terrain with full combat gear while the enemy was trying desperately to kill them. I had the latest gear, I carried a high tensile carbide trekking staff, was in excellent physical shape, and very lucky to escape unscathed. I called to Tangie and he appeared on the north end of the slope, safe and sound. I should have waited for him.

When we got to the van, I realized the snapshot camera was missing. Tangie waited while I went back to the place where I fell. Using the old scout trick of following broken twigs, I found the camera with the pictures of Tangie holding Pope's Medal of Honor citation.

Tangie and I climbed several peaks in the Umurbrogol across from Pope Hill. Along the way Tangie pointed out Wildcat Bowl, Death Valley, the China Wall, the Five Brothers, and countless caves. We found live grenades on Hill 300 (GPS: N 07° 00.689', E 134° 14.160'), including pineapple and rifle-launched types. Elsewhere in the Umurbrogol we found mortar rounds, gun emplacements, wheels and a rice bowl very close to another cave. At one point, my trekking staff hit metal. I initially thought it might have been ordnance but thankfully it turned out to be a mortar support platform. We left the live grenades behind and headed down the hill very carefully before we went over to the Five Sisters and the observation deck.

It was very emotional to climb Hill 260 (GPS: N 07° 00.726', E 134° 14.137'), the place where my father was wounded by bayonet while lowering Bangalore torpedoes into a cave opening. He described the circumstances and his recovery:

> We received orders to report to the Beachmaster. We reported as Marines, and were directed up to the command post. The beach was a mess. The Japanese had targeted the invasion and destroyed amphibious troop carriers during the first wave. The Beachmaster said he needed us to clear the beach landing zones of war debris that littered the waters. There was a severe shortage of demolitions people.

Our assignment was far from over. After our beach duty, we were assigned to help "K" Company, 3rd Battalion, 1st Marines for a day and a half, then transferred to 2nd Battalion, 7th Marines. Our duty was to help advance on Umurbrogol Mountain, "Bloody Nose Ridge." My job, as a demolitions expert, was to take Bangalore torpedoes and satchel charges to blow up the caves where the Japanese had hunkered down. The "torpedoes" were 5' long, 3" diameter pipes with explosives and primacord. We had to climb the ridge and lower torpedoes into the openings, sealing the caves on one end. It was dangerous duty as I concentrated on the difficult task with limited rifle support when suddenly someone shouted, "Here they come!" I turned around to see the Japanese soldiers on top of us. It was close-quarters, fierce rifle fighting, finally ending in hand-to-hand combat. We got the best of them, but a Japanese bayonet seriously wounded me. I was 19 years old with the three stripes of a buck sergeant. I didn't think I would live to see my 20th birthday later in September.

They shipped me out to Guam and then on to Hawaii, where I was admitted to the Aeia Heights Hospital. I was dirty and wounded, but I could walk and went to breakfast. They wouldn't let me in the mess hall. A corpsman went down for some fresh clothes and brought back some food for me.

I was in the hospital through Christmas. My parents received a letter from the Red Cross and a visit from a chaplain telling them that I was missing in action.

Shortly thereafter, I was in the hospital ward that treated shattered limbs. In an unbelievable coincidence, Dr. Sidney Derow was the physician in charge. He had set my ankle when I was a boy. A car had hit me on my bicycle while delivering newspapers in my hometown of Newton, Massachusetts. He wrote to his wife, who relayed the message to my parents that I was alive and in the hospital.

There was trouble with my thyroid gland. I learned later that the residue of explosives, a familiar aroma that I had grown to like, adversely affected the thyroid. I was treated with radioactive iodine. During my hospital stay, I befriended Frank Scavuso, a PFC who had been clobbered on Guam while serving with an engineer battalion. [13]

As rugged as it was to climb together with Tangie, it is difficult to imagine how anyone survived Peleliu in combat. Most of the terrain was denuded in 1944 by the artillery barrage and bombing, but we couldn't move more than a few feet through the dense growth without looking for alternate routes. Tangie disappeared into one of the many caves littering the Umurbrogol. It had a narrow opening with a honeycomb of tunnels. I followed and was astonished to see its curved passageways and escape routes. I took one photo in thick growth and realized it was precariously close to a sheer drop-off with deadly limestone rocks waiting below for the unwary.

The experience was unlike anything else in my life. I felt an eerie presence. The haunting jungle noises echoed the sounds of twenty thousand fighters locked in do-or-die combat. There was a propelling force that motivated me after I had mastered the proper way to climb and descend. Tangie let me go off on my own while he paused on a plateau off the road to the Five Sisters. I hiked on and climbed the 114 steps to the observation deck where there is a clear view of the China Wall, Death Valley and the White and Orange Beaches. At the monument erected by the 323rd Infantry of the U. S. Army, a bright green gecko greeted me poised at the top of the metal lettering and helped to narrate the video by climbing

Cave hidden in the Umurbrogol Mtns. (Photo © 2004 Patrick Finelli)

Umurbrogol Mtn., Five Sisters. (Photo © 2004 Patrick Finelli)
GPS: N 07° 00.732', E 134° 14.132'

Umurbrogol, 1944. (Photo Courtesy Gabe Ineichen)

115

Author on observation deck, Umurbrogol Mtns., SW towards Anguar.

Beaches from the Umurbrogol. (Photo © 2004 Patrick Finelli)

down slowly as if deliberately pointing out the words, "Lest We Forget Those Who Died." Tangie arrived shortly thereafter and we took pictures of each other on the observation deck. Then he walked down the stairs while I searched with my GPS to locate Hill 260.

Although the hills were honeycombed with caves, I found one reinforced cave near the spot my father had described within sight of the sea high on the Umurbrogol. It was made out of a natural limestone formation with concrete buttressing the opening. My emotions got the best of me and, as Dad suggested later, I could practically see his fingerprints. I wanted to linger at this spot that was the scene of a pivotal moment in his life history. I thought of my own mortality and all of those sons who were not born because their would-be fathers perished on Peleliu. I touched the entrance of the cave that had been reduced to rubble sixty years ago. It was difficult turning away to begin my descent. After about fifty footsteps I climbed back up for one more visit and literally broke down in tears. Finally, I was ready to go back to the present, the world of sunny skies and tropical temperatures. Tangie was waiting. We sipped from our water bottles and walked down the rest of the way to the van. We drove back in silence to our cottage at the Storyboard where we knew divers would be returning from their daily excursion. The van became a decompression chamber for me before re-entering the world of living human beings after a transcendent moment touching and feeling the past.

One of the best tips I received from Phil Orr was to take Gatorade®. I brought two bottles from Malakal, but Tangie stopped at three different stores on Peleliu and each one had cold beverages and ice cream. I would never have recognized them as stores since they looked like every other building except for the sign marked "Open." Although a can of Orange Crush® or Fanta® was only sixty cents, Tangie would always try to bargain the price down. He was my friend and watched out for me out of respect and loyalty for Everett Pope and my own father whom he had never met.

Diving Truk Lagoon taught me a great deal about important

strategies and outcomes in the Pacific during World War II. The sunken freighters I explored there were filled to the brim with ammunition, heavy artillery, torpedoes, hemispherical beach-type mines, tanks, bulldozers, trucks, mortar rounds, cordite, and the ubiquitous sake bottles.

On Peleliu, I saw sake bottles recycled into land mines—Molotov cocktails with nitrate embedded in concrete blocks with cord detonators. We explored many caves and tunnels, including the thousand-man cave with numerous passages and rooms for ammunition and medical care. Souvenir hunters have taken much of the loot like glassware and mess kits, but there were mortar rounds, land mines and fuses. One of my digital videotapes shows bats flying right at us while Tangie held my HID dive light to illuminate the cave. The 10-volt, ionized gas lamp produced 12,500 watts of pure bright light.

Entering the thousand-man cave. (Photo by Tangie Hesus)

The Seabees deserve a lot of credit for rebuilding the islands I visited. On Peleliu, they built harbors, repaired the airport, and

118

essentially created an infrastructure for the island including roads, electricity, and a water-pumping station. My sister received some papers from the spouse of a patient who was a Seabee, and among them she found a clever poem:

Mortar rounds in thousand-man cave. (Photo © 2004 Patrick Finelli)

The Seabees
(author unknown)

We work like hell, we fight like hell,
and always come back for more,
The Navy's Advance Base Engineers -
on many a foreign shore.

On half the lousy islands
From here to Timbuktu,
You will find a hive of Seabees -
One hell of a fighting crew.
The Admiral dropped by to chat
just the other night.

He said, "Now boys, I know you work,
but you've also got to fight;
and if there's any trouble,
don't stop to don your jeans.
Just drop your tools, grab your guns,
And protect the damn Marines!"

Very few of the roads had street signs. When I suggested we should start a program for signage, Tangie said that the locals would throw them into the swamp. However, I was greeted with betel nut smiles and moving stories of displacement and return, thanks to the U.S. Armed Forces.

Tangie's uncle Teibo told me he was born in 1942 and the Japanese forced his family to leave Peleliu for Babeldoap in March 1944. His wife's name is Mayumi and the inn they own is popular with divers. Teibo chewed betel nut as we had an animated conversation in his kitchen dining area while Mayumi punched my Belau Air ticket for the next day's flight back to Koror.

Tangie showed me his hardbound edition of *The Assault on Peleliu* published by the 1st Marine Division. The book is the definitive account of the battle. Senator John McCain had been to Peleliu recently and his signature was on the same page Tangie asked me to autograph. I was honored to sign Tangie's book just below Senator McCain's name.

I showed Tangie an article published by the United States Naval Institute titled "The Bones of Nakagawa" about an expedition to discover the last command post of the Japanese colonel in charge of defending Peleliu. Tangie said that the group led by a fellow named Underwood did not ask permission and Peleliu's Governor, Jackson Ngiraingas, was upset about their visit and subsequent unauthorized removal of material from Nakagawa's cave in Death Valley. Peleliu protects its heritage and Tangie called them "thieves."

I'm still having a difficult time with the battlefield aspect of my research trip. I cannot visualize or understand how the Marines gained ground, except by sheer determination and willingness to

120

die for an incremental advance. Add in 115° F heat with only sand and hard corals for cover. The Marines were up against a fanatical, highly trained Manchurian-experienced defense force determined to die rather than surrender, hiding in impenetrable, reinforced caves with weapons and artillery. No one who was not there can possibly comprehend what it was like for those combat Marines to cross hundreds of yards in shallow water under withering enemy fire, establishing a beachhead before moving inland to take the airport and the strategic ground. No wonder the casualties were terribly high.

Peleliu is still extremely dangerous, but it looks benign from the air and sea in the 21st century. You can find tranquil lagoons and beaches, although White and Orange Beaches were not used for recreation as far as I could tell during my time there. I wondered why, and came to the conclusion that the invasion beach fringing reefs extend too far and are too shallow for swimming, especially at low tide. The hard corals are treacherous, and unexploded ordnance still makes it a dangerous place. I saw many locals swimming in the lagoons without surf, corals or debris of war, and others enjoying the amenities at Honeymoon Beach, on the eastern (Pacific) side of the island.

The juxtaposition of memory, history and the present state of the island created strong imagery in my mind, yet it is beyond my comprehension to try to understand how the Battle of Peleliu was won. If the Japanese had any air force or navy left, or if those supply ships from Chuuk had made it in February 1944 with more tanks, mines and ammunition, it might have been a different story. It is a challenge to come to grips with history and how it is written.

Some of the vets on the tour group in Malakal said that 2005 may be the last year that tourists will be permitted to visit Iwo Jima because the Japanese are expanding their naval base. There was no official word about closing access to Iwo Jima, it was just an educated guess by one of the veterans, and much of the historical tour information indicates that it may be true. I cannot believe the iconic memorial on Mt. Suribachi will soon be off-limits. I've written an e-mail of concern about this to Senator McCain since he is chair of the Veteran's Affairs committee in Congress.

When the day turned into late afternoon and the sun dropped slowly in the western sky, we left the Storyboard Resort and drove to the east side beaches, ending up at Honeymoon Beach (also called Purple Beach) and then the Peace Park to the north.

One day Tangie and I invited two divers, Cameron and Ashlie, along with Tangie's cousin Sisca Vogt and her husband John to join us for the fresh sea breeze and a relaxing end to the day. Sisca's maiden name is Remengesau; she is the younger sister of President Tommy Remengesau. The picture below was taken as we watched a turtle bobbing in the surf. It was strange for me to realize we were at a place where the Pacific Ocean was on the east and the Philippine Sea to the west. Tangie sat with Sisca at Honeymoon Beach wearing his new Tampa Bay Buccaneer jersey.

Tangie and Sisca at Honeymoon Beach. (Photo © 2004 Patrick Finelli)

I walked over to a bench in the shade to jot down some thoughts in my journal while the others enjoyed the moment. I was not tired or physically stressed despite the difficult climbs and hiking over the past few days. The physical conditioning program my father had recommended made a big difference. It wasn't easy by any stretch of the imagination, yet the veterans do it on those Military Historical Tours. Perhaps they go to the Marine Monument, the steps on the Five Sisters, the airport, the beaches, buildings, and museum. The artillery gun is near the LVTs. Climbing the hills through the dense brush of the jungle and negotiating the steep and dangerous terrain requires extra effort. I had to catch my breath more than a few times.

I asked Tangie before we left if he would take me back to White Beach 1 to walk on the hard corals at low tide again to get a sense of what confronted the landing troops. They had it the worst, but no one who was on this island at any time in 1944 faced anything but death. I don't know how my father made it until he was wounded on September 26. Perhaps it was because he was

Marine Memorial. (Photo © 2004 Patrick Finelli)

held in reserve with the 1st Pioneers in ships offshore after his beach recon swim with the UDTs and was not in the initial wave of assault troops. But he was quickly thrust into action because they needed demolition support to reduce the caves. He was there during the most ferocious "take no prisoners" fighting. Somehow he managed to survive. Otherwise, our family wouldn't exist today. My afternoon companions were gathered together sitting on a log and I joined them because I couldn't write another word.

The next day Tangie and I departed from Peleliu. As we took off from the airstrip, Shakespeare's words reverberated in my mind as I looked down upon the Horseshoe, the monuments, and the places my father did his duty on the beaches and the Umurbrogol below us. Although written for King Richard II and his England, a slight modification at the end of the speech aptly describes the impenetrable coral island and its place in the annals of the First Marine Division:

> This royal throne of kings, this scepter'd isle,
> This earth of majesty, this seat of Mars,
> This other Eden, demi-paradise,
> This fortress built by Nature for herself
> Against infection and the hand of war,
> This happy breed of men, this little world,
> This precious stone set in the silver sea,
> Which serves it in the office of a wall,
> Or as a moat defensive to a house,
> Against the envy of less happier lands,
> This blessed plot, this earth, this realm – *Peleliu*
> (*Richard II, Act* II, scene i, lines 40-50)

Footnotes

[1] Personal interview with Patrick L. Finelli, June 17, 2002.

[2] Harry Gailey, *Peleliu: 1944*, Baltimore: The Nautical & Aviation Publishing Company of America, 1983, p. 148.

[3] Landing Vehicle Tracked (LVT).

[4] Landing Craft Mechanized (LCM).

Flying back from Peleliu airfield over the Umurbrogol and Beaches, heading for Ngedebus and Koror over the Rock Islands. (Photo © 2004 Patrick Finelli)

[5] Landing Ship Transport (LST).

[6] Francis Fane, letter to Patrick L. Finelli, 1 March 1988.

[7] Harry Gailey, *Peleliu: 1944*, Baltimore: The Nautical & Aviation Publishing Company of America, 1983, p. 66.

[8] Francis Fane, letter to Patrick L. Finelli, 1 March 1988.

[9] Lt. Cmdr Draper L. Kauffman was given the assignment in June 1943 to organize the first UDT unit called CDU (Combat Demolitions Unit) number 1 in Ft. Pierce, Florida. On July 14, 1944 at Tinian, UDT Team 5 under Lt. Cmdr. Kauffman attempted a mine clearing but the weather and sea conditions forced abandonment of explosives and abort of the mission.

[10] ABLE is a code name. Team ABLE's sunken ship is mentioned in a February 17, 2001 letter written by Lt. Bill Flynn, a member of UDT-7 at Peleliu. He states that UDT-6 "went ahead with the work." Flynn's letters were published in the Summer 2004 issue of *Fire in the Hole* (UDT-SEAL Museum Association), pp. 7-8.

[11] Personal interview with Patrick L. Finelli, June 17, 2002.

[12] See appendix A for an interview with Major Pope, and appendix C for his Medal of Honor citation.

[13] Personal interview with Patrick L. Finelli, June 17, 2002.

chapter

Rock Island Adventures 8

I returned to the West Plaza in Malakal. The BBC channel wasn't working and only the Japanese stations were coming through. It didn't matter after an eventful stay on Peleliu and an exciting flight over the Rock Islands. We took off from the airfield in a twin engine Belau Air Islander piloted by Matt, a betel nut chewing Australian. Tangie sat two rows back and I took the co-pilot's seat. It was a clear day and I recorded the entire flight on digital video. Matt flew over the Umurbrogol Mountains as we left Peleliu and let me record the landing on Koror. He said if the landing was good I should send the DVD to his boss. It was one of the most feathery landings I'd ever experienced.

The day had started on Peleliu with a light breakfast at the Storyboard Resort—Spam and a Danish roll with a cup of tea. Tangie asked a fellow who worked at the Yellow Wall restaurant near the docks to ride with us to the airport and return the van.

The Peleliu terminal is not much more than a lean-to, open to the air with a roof and a large banyan tree shading it. We made a satirical video while we waited for the plane, scanning the shelter as we described the "baggage claim," "immigration," and "customs." It was all contained in an area not much larger than a bus stop.

Here are fifteen things I observed on Peleliu apart from the debris of war and reminders of the battle:

1. Coconuts fall from the trees and onto the roof of the cottage at regular intervals. The safe advice is to look up when you walk from your room to the dining hall.
2. The roosters crow at the break of dawn and throughout the day.

3. The roads are mostly dirt except for the downtown area where the main road is as good if not better than most U.S. cities.
4. There are few road signs. It would be a good idea for the authorities to place road signs, or at least directional arrows to make it easier to find your way despite Tangie's admonitions that the locals would tear them out and toss them away.
5. Wild chickens are everywhere and they run rapidly across the roads through the jungle. Please don't ask why.
6. Land crabs are also everywhere. We saw someone stop and pick one up for a home-cooked meal.
7. Coca Cola®, Fanta® Orange Soda, and Nestea® cost only sixty cents (USD). Gatorade is just a little more.
8. Breakfast and dinner are served in a communal hut at the Storyboard Resort. We always had an American breakfast and a Japanese dinner. The Japanese entrees consisted of fish, rice, vegetables, noodles, tuna, ginger, sauces, chicken, and banana crepes for dessert. Mayumi made sandwiches for lunch.
9. I skipped lunch on Saturday once I learned the ham was most likely Spam. Terry Etapa, a Boeing engineer from Seattle and expert diver, actually liked it, although his wife Susan didn't. Susan said it is a delicacy in Micronesia. I didn't know if she was kidding.
10. Tangie had a difficult time as a vegetarian since the basic food staples are meat and fish.
11. Although Tangie's van was falling apart, at least it got us around the island and never broke down.
12. I'm grateful that Tangie gave up other requests for tours to be my personal driver, translator and battlefield guide. He usually does this only for dignitaries—generals, senators and high-ranking officials.
13. The bugs were not as bad as I expected. I brought a bug shirt with a mesh hood and slept in it one night, but decided to use DEET bug spray the rest of the time.

14. We were supposed to fly to Anguar but flew directly from Peleliu back to Koror. Belau Air is very reliable if you work with local Palauans.
15. I photographed two churches: the Peleliu Evangelical Church and the Catholic Church. Sunday is the day for worship, but the Catholic Church was full whenever we passed it. The people have strong religious faith.

I was anxious to let my folks know about my visit to Peleliu and logged onto the computer in the hotel lobby to check e-mail and send them a note upon arrival back in Malakal. There were additional messages from my sister Chris, Phil Orr and Jeanne O'Neil, a neighbor and civic leader keeping me informed about the progress of our downtown revitalization project in Florida. Phil Orr had responded quickly to my note about what we saw on Peleliu and was anxious to explore the Avenger wreck on Pope Hill during his own trip scheduled for the end of June.

I walked to the dive shop to see which boat they scheduled for me the following day, and what time to expect the van to pick me up at the hotel. I was pleased to see that I was to be with Jonas on the dive boat *Tigershark*. The plan called for three dives: Saies Corner, Shark City and Ulong Wall. It promised to be another great day in paradise.

The next morning I had an early breakfast with Chris, the retired law enforcement officer from Sacramento whom I had met the previous week. He was still trying to book a trip to Peleliu, but continued to have little success in contacting Belau Air. He would share a new anecdote about Palau whenever I'd meet him for breakfast at the Red Rooster Café in the hotel. He said he enjoyed the company at Kramer's, a restaurant overlooking the sea. He raved about Kramer's sashimi and fish wrapped in banana leaf along with special menu items that often included a variety of cuisines ranging from Thai to Mexican food. Most of all, he liked the reasonable prices. Chris made a lot of friends there. He told me about the day the power went out because someone knocked over a telephone pole with a car, and about a truck in the water next to the Friendship Bridge. One of the locals jokingly told him it was the Palau carwash.

Chris had rented a car and offered to drive me the next day after my dives to bargain for storyboards carved by the inmates at the jail on Koror. He mentioned a bicycle shop that doubled as a jewelry store and said he'd take me there to shop for souvenir necklaces.

Antique glass beads (*Udoud*) serve as a valuable means of monetary exchange within and among the clans. It is an important element in Palauan culture to mark major clan events such as births, marriage and housewarming ceremonies with beads. I doubted whether we would find an authentic *lek* (necklace) or bracelet at the bicycle shop. The valuable beads come in different colors: large yellow or orange beads called *Bachel* and smaller ones named *Kldait*. There are blue and green beads with white specks and swirls.

Chris and I agreed to meet for lunch the following day, and take it from there. He suggested I just knock on his hotel room door when I got back. It sounded like a good idea, but everything hinged on when I returned from the dives. Little did I know that the next day I would return two hours later than planned.

After breakfast with Chris, I ran into a retired Air Canada and Belau Air pilot named Peter and his wife Joyce in the lobby while waiting for the van. He offered to drive me over to Sam's Tours dive shop.

Saies Corner was supposed to be a fantastic dive. It would be easy to become enthralled with the abundant sea life. Since the maximum depth might be near 130′, I decided to use compressed air. The MOD (maximum overall depth) for EANx 32 (Nitrox) was 111′ and I didn't want to put myself in jeopardy with potential oxygen toxicity.

Tom was my dive buddy for the next couple of days. He was an experienced and knowledgeable diver with a good sense of humor. He was from Marin County in California and had hundreds of dives under his weight belt. He liked to take his time underwater and we glided along the wall checking in with each other periodically. We saw king mackerel, triggerfish, purple queen anthias, pyramid butterfly fish, giant trevally, yellow tip fusiliers, and many sharks including gray reef and whitetip. We used our reef hooks at the corner to revel in the view.

It was so comfortable that I decided to put away my reef hook using a variation of the running eye knot where I made a series of overhand loops to shorten the line and make it easier to play out the next time I needed it. Every dive in Palau was a drift dive. However, I was so enraptured with the scenery and concentrating on tying the loops while drifting to the surface that I didn't keep an eye on my air gauge. I took a breath and the regulator felt tight. My air gauge indicated zero; there was no air left. Since I had already completed my safety stop, I signaled Tom that I was headed up to the surface to deploy my signal sausage and wait for the boat driver to pick me up.

Experienced divers sometimes make mistakes. While busy re-tying my reef hook line, I had violated a cardinal rule: check your air supply regularly. I surfaced and signaled the boat with the inflatable sausage and reflections from a metal mirror I carried in my BC pocket. It seemed to me that it was unusual to consume a full tank of air, but I was fine and never panicked at all. The dive boat driver noticed the empty tank when he removed my gear and there was not enough air left to purge the regulator clear. It had been my only compressed air dive since Chuuk.

Shark City was next on our itinerary for the day. The maximum depth was about 80 feet, making Nitrox a good choice for this dive. Afterward, we agreed that the site could be renamed "Turtle City" since we saw more turtles than sharks, although we did see a few whitetip sharks. I must have become jaded from seeing so many big animals in the sea. There was a strong current and it was a fine dive.

Time seemed to stand still during our surface interval. We pulled up in the shallows of Ulong Island alongside the ubiquitous Taiwanese snorkelers. Many of our divers took advantage of the shaded benches on the white, sandy beach for lunch and a mid-day siesta. The lavatory facilities were primitive. If you plan on stopping at Ulong, my advice is to leave your wetsuit behind and make sure you rinse off thoroughly on the way back to the boat from shore.

I overheard a young couple speaking a language that sounded familiar. I started a conversation using my rusty college conversational German, but when I spoke to them I realized their fluency was about the same level as mine. It turned out they were from Israel and he was studying architecture at the University of Frankfurt.

Ulong (or Oolong) Channel was a sensational dive. It was relatively shallow at 62 feet maximum and I used Nitrox again. There were schools of chevron barracuda, a huge goliath grouper and many sharks. The numerous gray reef and whitetip sharks pleased two Swiss and French photographers on board who begged the divemaster to take us where they were most likely to get pictures of the denizens of the deep.

Personally, I was more impressed with the strong current that ripped through a sandy cut in the reef. I couldn't fight it and just had to go with the flow. It was like a freight train. The only way to slow down was to find nooks and crannies among the corals or face backward into the current and kick. I used the reef hook when I wanted to linger.

There was an area off to one side at the end of one channel sheltered by some large coral formations. What did we see? Lo and behold—the nearly mythical giant clams of the far Pacific. They were larger in diameter than the length of my arm. I touched one shell and watched it close then open very slowly. What a thrill it was to see them at last.

I had plenty of air and perfectly neutral buoyancy. My dive buddy Tom had a little problem with his BC inflator valve "free flowing" (leaking air) and had to surface early. I stayed with our divemaster Jonas. The Israeli couple was not far behind.

Our boat returned to the dive shop late in the day and I saw Sam again. A couple of the divemasters liked the waterproof boat shoes I wore with bungee cord laces and antimicrobial and antibacterial inserts. The rugged, lightweight shoes had withstood the sharp corals of Peleliu. They suggested I show them to Sam.

Sam was suitably impressed, and gave me advice about how to deliver a FedEx package to Tangie. Since most addresses in Koror, including Sam's own business, used a post office box and FedEx doesn't ship to a P.O. Box, Sam said to use the same number and put "Main Street" next to it.

Sam's stalwart manager, Russelle Caraig, helped me arrange for Tangie to pick up the FedEx package when it eventually arrived in Koror. She was the only one I was able to contact with certainty. Sam's Tours is a first-class operation in my opinion. Although there were more novice divers than anywhere else on my journey, and I witnessed quite a few panic attacks and equipment breakdowns, Sam's staff handled it all with aplomb. Even experienced divers can have problems. I had mine when I neglected to check my air gauge, and my buddy Tom had a purge valve on his BC that was not repairable. He used a rental, but didn't fasten the strap securely and the tank fell out when he hit the water. All was not lost, though, as it was attached to his regulator and he quickly corrected it without missing out on the dive.

I had a tough time getting to sleep after our Ulong day. It felt like an infestation of fleas or gnats. The insects could be from the bats in the thousand-man cave on Peleliu, or Larry, the friendly dog at the Storyboard Resort; but it was more likely they had followed me from my mid-day visit to Ulong Island and its elevated outhouse. Those who stayed longer on Ulong said they saw large rats. I took a hot shower and rubbed down with isopropyl alcohol followed by DEET. I also decided to try the other bed.

Despite all of my preparation, I still couldn't get to sleep. I went downstairs to check e-mail on the public computers. It was somewhat of a shock to see Lisa, the young Filipina woman who worked at the front desk, in her pajamas sitting at the Japanese computer. I sat at the computer next to her and went about my own business. Suddenly, she burst into the familiar song "Happy Birthday." I didn't quite know what to make of it and a number of tag lines danced on the tip of my tongue: "Where's the party?" "When do we unwrap the presents?" and "Who's going to blow out the candles?" Discretion was the better part of valor. It turned out to be the birthday of the other night clerk. I finally made it upstairs about 2:30 A.M. in time to get some rest before diving Blue Corner for the last time on this trip.

The next day I was on the *Hammerhead* with Jonathan and Maggie. Our destination was the Blue Holes. Maggie, the young California blonde I met working in the dive shop my first day in Palau, and Jonathan, the self-described "little man, big fins, tall woman" Palauan were fantastic on our last day's diving excursion. Jonathan referred to technical divers as "Inspector Gadgets." Maggie and Jonathan both chewed betel nut. Blue Corner was also on the list since one novice diver had not been there yet. I wanted to do two dives and give my gear a good rinsing and time to dry before departure, but a third stop was planned.

Blue Holes is a must-dive in Palau. There were a lot of boats in the water around the site. The sea was flat like a pane of glass. Despite the flotilla of recreational dive boats, scuba divers moved in and out quickly. The site is slightly to the north of Blue Corner. We approached from the west through the largest of the four Blue Holes. The holes begin in the shallows, around 12 to 18 feet, and then lead into a spectacular cathedral-like space with rays of sunlight filtering through the crystal-clear water. One of the best views in the sea is to look up once you reached depth and revel in the scenic spectacle of divers in the flickering sunlight against the coral cavern walls. I reached a maximum depth of 92 feet.

Jonathan showed us the "Disco Clam." It appeared as if there was some sort of electrical charge inside the shell, like a spark between two wires or the static discharges from a Tesla coil. It looked like a colorful, miniature bolt of lightning. It is near the entrance of "The Temple of Doom," a cavern that begins at about 90 feet deep at the bottom of Blue Holes just north of Blue Corner. The name derives from the numerous turtle skeletons nearby. The sea turtles go there to die for an unknown reason. The divemaster told me that four cave divers lost their lives there a few years ago after becoming disoriented while exploring at greater depths.

There was a more recent diving accident in December 2003. Michael Norwood, an experienced British scuba diver and co-host of the History Channel series "Deep Sea Detectives," lost his life during a 250-foot dive to the *U. S. S. Perry*, a World War II wreck. The ship survived the bombing of Pearl Harbor, but went to the bottom on Sept. 13, 1944 after striking an underwater mine. The *Perry* was attempting to clear the mines for the Marine invasion at Peleliu. It is located in an area of strong currents and tremendous depths of over 240 feet near the island of Anguar. This wreck is for advanced technical divers only. Recreational scuba divers should adhere to the rule of 100-foot maximum depth, with occasional forays to greater depths only under controlled conditions while making sure to pay strict attention to their bottom time and decompression requirements.

There were two exits from the Blue Hole we explored, one small opening at about 82 feet and a larger opening just beneath it. Jonathan and I took the tricky upper swim-through and everyone else joined us after swimming under the arch below. We drifted with the wall on our left, a common refrain, and I sensed we were approaching Blue Corner, but air consumption required the group to make a safety stop and summon the boat captain to pick us up for a surface interval.

We approached Blue Corner from another direction than previously. I could never get too much of Blue Corner even though the action takes place at a relatively shallow 72' depth. The current was barely noticeable this time, and the dynamic action of the sea life is proportional to the strength of the current. Nevertheless, there were many blue line fusiliers, bar jack, big-eyed goatfish, and a Napoleon wrasse. We noticed quite a few sleeping whitetip sharks on our way back and a nice moray while we were doing a safety stop. I came up with a lot of Nitrox left and wish I could have stayed down forever. It was my last real dive of the trip.

Peleliu was clearly visible during our approach to Blue Holes, Blue Corner, during our diving intervals and final departure from the site. I kept my thoughts to myself, but I knew now what was there. The nature of actual combat remained a mystery to me, shared only by those who have experienced it themselves. There was tension in my heart between the beauty of the final dives and how profoundly the sight of that island in the sea affected me.

I was anxious to get back to Malakal where Chris was waiting with the car for our jailhouse journey and shopping spree. However, the French and Swiss divers wanted to take photos at Jellyfish Lake, so we stopped on the way back for our third "dive" of the day.

It was a long climb up and down a hill to the lake on the other side. Trees with poisonous sap that can burn the skin surrounded the rocky, hilly climb bordered with a rope along the trail to the lake. Scores of tourists from Taiwan swarmed the narrow path and filled the lake, swimming together in their life jackets holding foam rubber flotation devices with their snorkels and masks firmly attached. I put on my own mask, snorkel and fins and kicked hard to get ahead of the crowd looking for the sunniest spot.

The jellyfish stranded in a marine lake on Eil Malik Island are an evolutionary oddity. They have lost their sting over generations due to the lack of predators. There were two species of land-locked white (or moon) and translucent pink jellyfish (*Mastigias*) swimming frantically. The schools of jellyfish follow the sun's movement across the sky because they evolved from stinging their prey to nourishing themselves by processing green algae through photosynthesis. The energetic jellyfish soon surrounded me.

I reached out to briefly stop one's movement and its texture felt like silicon, soft and rubbery. More Taiwanese tourists arrived as I was leaving. I made another mental note to suggest that the dive shops stagger the snorkel tours so the divers on afternoon surface intervals will have more breathing room.

A woman on the boat, Carol, who lives with her husband Dave in Singapore, tried chewing betel nut while we were waiting at the Eil Malik dock. Jonathan had his kit that no Palauan would be without: an empty Elmer's glue bottle filled with a white powder made from heating the limestone coral and grinding it, an ample supply of betel nuts, and a mint-tasting leaf to wrap it up before placing in the mouth. Some chewers put tobacco or break up parts of a cigarette to place inside. Carol described her reaction in detail and asked someone to take a picture for posterity showing her red tongue and gums. It was a fitting end to a sunny day in Palau.

Despite enjoying the "must-see" landlocked jellyfish, I was slightly irritated that the desire of one individual named Brian, the same person who needed a course in night diving etiquette the week before, single-handedly forced the stop at Jellyfish Lake. It set my personal schedule back a few hours. However, Chris was waiting patiently in his room at the West Plaza when I got back. We drove to the jail where I bargained with the trustee before purchasing three storyboards for my parents, my sister and myself. Then we drove over to the bike repair shop and jewelry store, called "Gift Shop Yolt," where I picked up a Rock Island necklace as a memento.

As soon as I got back to the hotel, the phone rang at the front desk. It was Tangie. He had left a message in the morning, but I received it at 5:30 P.M., and he wanted to get together for dinner. We ate at the Palm Bay Bistro across from the hotel. We discussed plans for a storyboard on which to place my father's dog tag and wording for an engraved dedication plaque I would send upon returning home. Tangie agreed to make the arrangements for someone to carve the storyboard. I gave him extra money to cover his expenses and thanked him profusely for his efforts. It was an early night since I wanted to make sure I could pack all of my equipment, clothes and souvenirs for departure at midnight the following day.

My last day in Malakal was a leisurely one. Chris and I went to lunch at the Bottom Time Bar & Grill at Sam's Tours. We noticed a picture of a large yacht named *Tatoosh* on the wall in the outdoor bar/restaurant. The waiter confirmed our suspicions. It belonged to Microsoft co-founder Paul Allen. The yacht had the two helicopter pads, a 40' sailboat on davits and another power boat. The waiter said, "Allen sent the vessel to Palau and many of us worked on board while it was here. He joined the ship for some water sport fun after it had arrived."

We asked for more details, and he told us about Allen's Captain, Richard Bridge (an appropriate name for the skipper of a ship). I remembered that my friends John and Lisa Holloway had photographs on display in their houses in Orlando and Antigua from many cruises taken with Captain Bridge when he was Captain of the *WindSurf*, years before he was offered his position with Allen. Captain Bridge is a professional. He and his crew respected the confidentiality that Mr. Allen requires and never revealed their next port of call. The waiter told us the Microsoft billionaire arrived on his Boeing 767 (his other jet is a 757) based in Seattle (or Allentown as Susan Crane said at dinner on Peleliu).

I sampled Chris's barracuda sashimi at lunch. Sam didn't want me to leave because he said I brought the good weather. As my sister Chris would say, "It was meant to be."

chapter

Aftermath 9

The flight back from Palau was exhausting. It took twenty-two hours of flight time, not including layovers, across the International Date Line. The first two boarding passes from Palau to Guam and Guam to Hawaii, were marked a day later than the boarding pass from Hawaii to Houston. As I flew east, I went back in time. I saw the sun rise twice. I could have stopped in Hawaii for a few days, but I wanted to get back to my Florida house so my parents could return to Boston in time to attend their granddaughter Erin's confirmation ceremony.

We only had time to spend a day together looking at the videotapes from the trip. It was a treat to eat home cooking again, and my parents had filled the refrigerator and freezer with plenty of food. I was glad they were able to share my spontaneous narrative and feelings about the journey while my body's metabolism began the slow process of catching up from being "worlds away" in time and place. The 15-hour time change had taken its toll and I couldn't do much of anything for several days.

Something about me had changed. As someone who grew up in the 1960s and the Vietnam era, this journey had a profound influence on me, eliciting the utmost respect for the sacrifices that were made. It took a tremendous effort for our country to go from the attack on Pearl Harbor to victory in the Pacific.

I called my sister Chris after my parents flew home and tried to maintain my composure while describing what I had seen on Pelcliu. The horrific scenes described in the books and monographs written by Falk, Gailey, Gayle, Hallas, Hough, Hunt and Sledge infused my thoughts and emotions. You can learn a lot from the books, but there is nothing like experiencing what the limestone feels like under your feet, climbing the steep ridges, and descending into the damp isolation of a fortified cave.

139

I had felt a mixture of anticipation and apprehension during the boat ride that took me to Peleliu for the first time. I had been overcome with emotion and awe. A question resonated within me throughout my visit: "How did anyone survive this?" The Battle of Peleliu was incredibly bloody. The Japanese strategy was delay-and-bleed: slow the Marines down and take as many casualties as you can before dying. American forces had no idea how heavily fortified the island was. They were told it was going to be a walkover, "quick but rough"[1] in the pre-invasion words of General William Rupertus. It became a drawn-out battle of attrition. Both sides fought hard. It was a matter of who was going to survive.

No one can imagine what it was like for those Marines that invaded Peleliu. I couldn't begin to understand what it must have been like for my father to observe his 20th birthday on that island as he faced a lethal, suicidal force bent on killing as many Marines as possible without any real hope of victory. The debris of war on Peleliu bears witness to the catastrophic losses in the "meat grinder," and underscores the brutal nature of war and the fragility of this earthly life in ferocious and fatal combat.

The vestiges of war remain prominent throughout Micronesia today. Peleliu is idyllic, yet replete with physical reminders of great suffering inflicted during the heated, visceral battle. Tanks, mortar rounds, assault vehicles and wrecked planes litter the landscape. Each day you see shells, shards of metal, and more war debris on the beaches. You never know what the tide will bring in.

It was dangerous and highly technical to dive among the torpedoes, mines and artillery shells that remained underwater in Chuuk Lagoon. I was stunned by what I saw. Among the twisted steel beams and charred shipwrecks, I noticed a fragile teacup or porcelain bowl, untouched by the violent fury that brought them to the sea floor sixty years ago. The juxtaposition of these weapons of war with a fragile china bowl, mess kits, slippers, and glasses is sobering. It was like visiting a memorial, a graveyard of the Pacific. For me, it was a somber and moving experience.

This journey meant more to me than the places that I went

and what I did once there. Oddly, it was not difficult to hand my father's dog tag over to Tangie. My feelings upon giving up the aluminum tag dad wore in the war were counterbalanced by the knowledge that this was what he wanted. Although the chain around my neck had lost its talisman, I replaced it with a necklace featuring a piece of the Rock Islands for the flight home. I can never replace the experience of visiting the battle sites where he served. For my father, Peleliu happened sixty years ago. He did his duty and moved on, although it will always be part of his military history and inner life.

Once I sufficiently recovered from jet lag, I contacted Bill Raynor, Director of The Nature Conservancy for Micronesia, and shared my observations regarding the ecosystem of Palau. He answered promptly and forwarded my concerns to TNC's Palau Country Director, David Hinchley, and Dr. Andrew Smith, Director, Pacific Island Countries Coastal Marine Program. He told me that Palau had recently passed an anti-shark-finning bill, which was the first in Micronesia. He concluded by saying, "We are dedicated to working with the locals out here to make sure that the islands of Micronesia will be jewels in the Pacific for years to come."[2]

David Hinchley quickly followed with a detailed e-mail about shark-finning and other issues in Palau. He provided further details about the Palau Congress revising its foreign fishing legislation to banning shark-finning in September 2003, and he mentioned that government agencies have been taking a strong line against the practice. The revised legislation also bans all fishing for sharks within Palau's management zone, extends the zone further offshore (from 12 miles to 50 miles) and provides for much larger fines.

He mentioned recent law enforcement efforts and the current debate:

> Over recent months two boatloads of shark Division of Fish and Wildlife Protection enforcement officers seized fins. Both of these boatloads of fins were burned as a public statement, and the issue has been getting a lot of publicity locally and internationally. There is, however, pressure from the fishing industry to exempt three companies that had existing fishing

agreements in place when the law was passed from the legislation (they were half-way through 5-year agreements and they claim that the commercial viability of their operations has been severely impacted by the change) and a bill to this effect has been introduced to Congress.

This will be debated over the coming months and the various agencies involved in conservation and fisheries management are currently seeking to influence this debate to make sure that the provisions of the legislation are not weakened while recognizing the existing rights of the fishing companies. We at TNC are putting our main efforts into establishing a network of marine protected areas for Palau working together with the general fisheries legislation for the overall conservation of Palau's marine resources. [3]

David Hinchley also addressed the impact of tourism in the Rock Islands:

The issue you raise about snorkeling in Jellyfish lake and elsewhere has also come up for discussion fairly recently. Koror State has, over the last couple of years (with our assistance) been working on a comprehensive management plan for the Rock Islands and Southern Lagoon area. The plan is now in draft form and should be finalized in the next month or so. The issue of congestion is being addressed to some extent in the plan and a discussion paper of possible options for better control of snorkeling was recently presented to the Koror State Governor for consideration. The tour operators themselves are also concerned about the issue. Another initiative under the management plan is a tour guide certification and training program currently under development that will also deal with issues like this. So hopefully the issue will be able to be successfully addressed. [4]

I spoke with Everett Pope by telephone one Sunday afternoon and sent him the pictures of Tangie holding his Medal of Honor citation. He wrote a nice letter back saying, "The jungle does grow, doesn't it?" and asking for a copy of the article "The Bones of Nakagawa." [5] I'm looking forward to meeting him in person soon.

Terry Etapa, one of the scuba divers on Peleliu and fellow guest at the Storyboard Resort along with his wife Susan, sent an e-mail to say that one of his co-workers at Boeing in Seattle plans on researching his uncle's experiences on Peleliu. Terry was also kind enough to have glanced through my draft chapter on the Web and corrected the spelling of important Palauan names.

I asked Cliff at Odyssey Adventures to forward a note to Cara and Lenny, the owners of *Truk Odyssey*, letting them know about Arthur Tewasiliig, the Chukese student studying in the States. They replied with an e-mail that made me yearn to return soon. While landlocked divers like me dream of the extraordinary adventures and amenities on their fabulous liveaboard yacht, they were looking forward to a much-needed vacation on Guam for their 5th wedding anniversary. I hope they enjoy their stay amid familiar shops and restaurants as much as I enjoyed their hospitality.

I sent a FedEx package to Tangie with the picture of him holding Pope's citation folio, two 4 x 6 pictures of Tangie and Sisca sitting at Honeymoon Beach, the engraved plaque for my father's dog tag storyboard along with eight stainless steel screws, an application for the 1st Marine Division reunion in August with a special Peleliu section, and a copy of "The Bones of Nakagawa." Russelle at Sam's Tours checked and let me know that Tangie had picked it up. Tangie sent an e-mail about the progress of the storyboard carving for my father's dog tag.

Maria McGlynn, the videographer at Yap divers, notified me that Yap was hit badly by Typhoon Sudal a few weeks after I left, delaying the completion of her video on Yapese culture. I learned that Bill Acker and his crew at the Manta Ray Bay Hotel had discovered a World War II landing craft with a bomb on board. Eventually, it will be another exciting dive site.

Marty Hicks sent the *Life* magazines he promised and we exchanged e-mails. Ironically, Captain Hunt, the company commander for the assault under impossible conditions on The Point beachhead at Peleliu, became managing editor for *Life* magazine during the 1960s and covered events from John F. Kennedy's assassination to the Beatles.

Chris, the retired law enforcement officer from Sacramento I had met at the West Plaza in Malakal, gave me his e-mail address, but I have not been able to get a message through to him and I

143

have tried several iterations of the letters and numbers scrawled on a boarding pass.

Diane Kuebler and John Edwards, dinner companions at The Taj and members of the military historical tour group, have kept in touch. John has helped me to understand significant details about weapons used on Peleliu.

Phil Orr sent periodic updates during his June sojourn to Saipan, Peleliu and Guam, including his discovery of new locations of weapons, caves and human remains.

I've had several conversations with Gabe Ineichen who sent me 118 scanned photos taken during the Battle of Peleliu in 1944. He placed a notice in "The Old Breed" newsletter offering to share his CDs with veterans of the battle. Gabe attended the 60th anniversary of the Peleliu invasion on September 15, 2004.

Rob Amaral has corresponded frequently with me about his uncle, Sergeant Ed Amaral, the leader of the first squad of Marines to reach the Peleliu airfield. He quoted from an article in the *Brockton Enterprise* with a quote from Captain John W. Holland, Amaral's commanding officer, indicating that uncle Ed walked upright in front of his men directing their fire while Japanese mortar shells were landing and machine gun fire sprayed the beach. Holland said, "Sgt. Amaral never hit the deck once. I saw him knock out one Japanese pillbox as he advanced."

Mike Dunn of the *Tampa Tribune* wrote a superb story about my trip, published in the Sunday edition on Memorial Day weekend.[6] It was followed by an outpouring of sentiment and shared experiences from daughters, sons, nephews and nieces of men who fought on Peleliu.

Linda Frank's father, Eugene Michael Doyle, served with the 1st Marines and kept a journal that she transcribed after his death in 2000. He lived in Memphis, Tenessee where he enlisted after graduation from Christian Brothers High School. Linda is a realtor in Tampa. She said, "I wished I had asked him more questions about the war, but like so many of his generation it was just something he didn't talk about." Her father's journal contains his observations while on Cape Gloucester including "men getting the

Bronze Star" for recovering bodies from the wreckage of a B-24.

Linda's father indicated the men had learned on August 4th that they were headed for Palau and were told on August 15th that the island of Peleliu was the actual destination. Only the Marines knew. His journal mentions Bob Hope's show on Pavuvu with Frances Langford, Jerry Colonna, Patty Thomas and Bill Goodwin. Hope was in Banika with a USO unit when a colonel asked him to fly down for the extra show. Each performer had to fly in a separate light plane with a pilot and land on a road. More than 15,000 Marines greeted them on the baseball field and lined the road after the show. It created a lasting memory for the men and for Bob Hope:

> Four months later I was asked to bring some entertainers to dedicate a new surgical amphitheater at Oak Knoll Hospital in Oakland, California. We did a show for the people they packed into that amphitheater. Afterward the colonel doctor in charge said, "I hope you'll go through the wards and say hello." In the first ward, a kid in bed stuck out his hand. He said, "Pavuvu!" "First Marine Division?" I asked. "Yes," he said. "Every kid in this ward is from the First Marines."[7]

Sgt. Doyle landed on Orange Beach 3. He writes about a mortar shell missing his unit by 15 yards, as well as sharp-shooting snipers, heavy artillery, land mines, ammo dumps exploding, a Corsair crashing on the edge of the reef and a buddy killed by the accidental discharge of an army lieutenant's .45 caliber pistol.

Deborah Mitchell, a colleague at the university, wrote a note to say that her father was a Marine in the Battle of Peleliu. She found the names and passage dates of all six ships that her father was on from the time he shipped out of San Diego. He went to New Caledonia, Guadalcanal, Palau, Peleliu, and Okinawa. She wanted to find out if he was in the group that hit White Beach or Orange Beach. Deborah's father drove an amphibious landing craft, and she said he never wanted to talk much about it. She told me she had a number of photos from the islands. I'm looking forward to meeting her and seeing if we can determine when and where the photos were taken.

Much to my surprise, Martha J. Fry, newsroom editor for the *Tampa Tribune*, wrote to say her uncle, PFC Alonzo Austin Ford, died on Peleliu in October 1944. She grew up with stories of her "Uncle Lonnie." Her father passed away last year. She expressed regret that she had not been able to tell anyone about her uncle's sacrifice on Peleliu.

Juliana Gittler, a reporter with *Stars and Stripes* in Tokyo, interviewed me before and after traveling to Peleliu.

Tony Ippolito telephoned to talk about his brother Johnny who was with the 81st Wildcats.

Jim Rosencutter contacted me about his service as Captain's Radio Operator aboard the *U.S.S. Pinckney*, a troop transport before the battle and then a hospital ship. He mentioned two fellow sailors named Richins and Richmond who worked with the doctors on deck tending to the seriously wounded. The troops went over the side on cargo nets down to the landing vehicles prior to the assault, and the wounded were evacuated to his ship. He saw a lot of wounds caused by "knee mortars," a compact weapon, and said that before the invasion the island looked barren and desolate. One Japanese shell exploded fifty feet from his ship, knocking him across the deck, causing a concussion and wounding him with shrapnel over his left eye. When I spoke with him, he was in good spirits rebuilding a family home. He was an eyewitness to history. Like many veterans, he said that his records didn't indicate many of his transfers and he never received the medals his commanding officer had recommended. Above all, he wanted to commend the medical personnel on the hospital ship for their tireless duty attending serious wounds suffered by the U.S. Marines.

I went to a diving festival in Bonaire in June 2004. I told a few of my fellow divers about my visit to Peleliu. Rob Neft, a scuba buddy and friend for over thirty years, spoke with his father about it when he returned to California. He discovered that his father had spent a night on Peleliu during World War II while with the Medical Administration Corps (MAC). At the time, he was on his way from New Guinea to the Philippines. Lieutenant Sam Neft shot about 1,200 feet of film, mostly in the Philippines. His film shows the nose of the DC-3 transport on the Peleliu airfield with men gathered around the plane. His father slept under the wing of the plane and said he could hear the Marines fighting in the hills. He had to shoot the film and then send it to Australia for processing and censoring. The only shots that were excised were of skulls and skeletons. The War Office said that particular content represented atrocities and could not be shown.

On Memorial Day I attended the dedication of a "Blue Star" plaque and tribute patio, having engraved a brick for my father. There were a few other World War II combat veterans including a Bataan survivor. There was a young Marine in the row in front of me. He stood ramrod straight saluting the colors during the entire time the guard brought the flags forward until they returned to the reception area. He is the son of our chief of police. Tony told me his son would ship out to Iraq soon in the 2nd Marine Division, 1st Marines.

I thought about that young Marine and how perfect he looked, fit and trim, in his dress uniform. He represented the Corps like no other military man there. He was in a class by himself, at the peak of physical and mental readiness. Everyone should be proud of him and his commitment, but it is a shame that young men have to go to war, and front lines are everywhere in the changing battlefield of today's world. Of course, we can say that about other places and other wars.

This book is about my father's service, but it is important to mention those on both sides of my family who served their country in the military. My grandfather Frank Finelli joined the Navy and earned his citizenship by serving in World War I. There is an engraved brick listing his WWI Naval duty at his grave. He lived in Newton, Massachusetts for 74 years.

In addition to my father's Marine Corps duty, his older brother Tony served in the Navy aboard LST 871.[8] Among my uncle's ports of call were Chuuk and Guam, where he relentlessly searched until he found my father in the hospital. One of my Dad's most memorable recollections from the war was to see my uncle walking into his ward unannounced.

Radarman Anthony Finelli (back row, second from left) and crewmates
on deck, 1945.

Radarman Anthony Finelli

Uncle Tony also wrote an essay with his observations while sailing into Nagasaki after the devastation of the atomic bomb. Uncle Tony received his Ph.D. in chemistry from the University of Pennsylvania and held patents for materials used in artificial heart valves and prosthetic limbs. Tony's son Frank graduated from West Point and retired from the Army at the rank of colonel. Robert N. Finelli, my father's younger brother, served in the Air Force. His duties included base operations and flight control in Wiesbaden, Germany in the 1950s.

Members of my mother's immediate family also served with distinction. Her brother, whom we call Uncle Bud (James DiPalma), earned the rank of major as an Air Force pilot. He flew a Douglas C-124 Globemaster to Thule, Greenland and elsewhere during the Cold War. He served in the Vietnam War flying reconnaissance

James J. DiPalma, USAF in 1954

aircraft similar to the Helio Courier, a STOL aircraft designed for short takeoffs and landings on less than ideal surfaces. He flew four engine jets after his tour in Vietnam. Like many combat veterans, he doesn't like to talk about his own wartime exploits.

However, during one of my regular visits with him, he told me about assembling a new plane without a torque wrench and taking it for a test flight prior to dangerous reconnaissance missions over Laos. He talked about his fellow flyboys, and his visit to the touring Vietnam memorial. More than a few of his close buddies didn't make it home.

Our cousin, Captain Robert F. DiPalma USN (Ret), has had a stellar military career as a navigator and naval officer in Hawaii and Micronesia. His son Matt was a Marine and also lives in Florida.

My sister Chris has traced the ancestry of my mother's maternal grandfather back to the age of Shakespeare in England. Our great grandfather's lineage is of Puritan descent beginning with William Haskell landing in the ship *Elizabeth* on Cape Ann Side in 1634, known today as Gloucester, Massachusetts. Later, his descendants moved to Kennebec County, Maine where a distant relative and Civil War veteran was buried in 1865 in the older west part of Kennebec's Togus National Cemetery. We have identified English and Irish ancestors that fought in the Civil War (Bull Run and Antietam), the War of 1812, the Revolutionary War (Bunker Hill) and the Colonial Wars.

The Battle of Peleliu has many parallels to America's war against terrorism. The hidden caves in the limestone cliffs recall the caves of Afghanistan at Zhawar Kili and the tribal regions of Pakistan. Another deadly similarity is a fanatical enemy willing to die rather than surrender while inflicting the greatest number of casualties using a defense-in-depth without any hope of victory.

War is not heroic, but there are courageous acts. Few of the veterans think of themselves as heroes. They give praise to their buddies and the other soldiers with them in the foxholes. You almost have to pry it out of the surviving veterans to get them to say anything. The same was true for my own father.

There is much more to report and this narrative just scratches the surface. This story comes from a son's eyes, looking back into the past and across oceans to try to come to grips with those who served their country and wanted nothing more than to "do their

150

duty." One veteran who went to the Iwo Jima commemoration said, "I can tell you a lot about weapons and strategies, but you will never understand combat unless you have been there." This is the same response I heard from my father when I interviewed him about his experiences.

My sister works supervising hospice volunteers who care for people who are dying. One 82-year old veteran told her about his Seabee experiences and he was genuinely moved when she told him how much respect I have for the work they did on Peleliu

It seemed fitting that the veterans gathered in Washington, D.C. for the dedication of the World War II Memorial as I sat at my keyboard writing this final chapter while watching it on television. The memorial site covers over seven acres around a restored rainbow fountain with two pavilions at each end representing the Atlantic and Pacific theaters. There are 56 pillars around the perimeter representing a state or territory. A bronze rope connects the state monuments symbolizing the unity of our country at war. Twenty-four bas-relief sculptures depict scenes on the front lines and in the factories and farms on the home front.

There are 4,000 gold stars on a wall. Each one represents 100 military deaths. The tradition of blue stars on a flag displayed in the windows of families with sons or daughters in the military began with the American War Mothers in 1917 during World War I. Tragically, many sewed gold stars over the blue in tribute to their loved ones killed in action, becoming "Gold Star Mothers."

The dedication of the memorial was the largest ticketed event (140,000) ever held in our nation's capital. It may have been the largest assembly of octogenarians in history. Of the 16 million who served, only about 4 million are still alive at an average age of eighty-one. World War II veterans are dying at a rate of over 1,000 a day.

Tom Brokaw praised the achievements of the "Greatest Generation," not only in winning the war, but after the war was over saying, "You gave us new industry, new art, new science and unparalleled prosperity." Former Senator Bob Dole said, "What we dedicate today is not a memorial to war. Rather, it is a tribute to

151

the physical and moral courage that makes heroes out of farm and city boys, that inspires Americans of every generation to lay down their lives for people they'll never meet." Senator Dole observed in an interview that he saw a lot of daughters and granddaughters there with the veterans.

I thought of my sister Chris and how she pressed me to find a way to pay tribute to my father's duty in World War II. She was the one who gave me the motivation and I would never have written this story without her. My father is content to live with our mother, his wife of 56 years, surrounded by four children and three granddaughters. My father made a significant contribution to his country and our family's heritage as a duty-bound member of the Marine Corps in war and in peace through his longtime career as a creative, patent-holding engineer. My father and his fellow servicemen returned to a grateful nation. They knew the precious value of life and family values.

My father's enlistment papers indicate he signed up for the "duration," which must mean he was committed until we either won the war or he died valiantly. Fortunately for us, Dad came home again with a mildewed duffel bag and his memories. He has never been one to attend reunions or celebrate his achievements. He lives a quiet, peaceful life and swims an hour every other day.

Thanks to the sacrifices and support of our parents, my siblings and I have earned advanced university degrees and established our own careers. Despite the inevitable trials and tribulations of adolescence and occasional generational differences, we recognize their contributions and all of those who served in World War II. They built our houses and started businesses, making a better life for their offspring. They lived through depression and war to create a great and prosperous nation. We are the beneficiaries of the legacy they created for us. Let us not forget those who died, and those who live on in our hearts and minds, ghosts of an island 9,000 miles away.

Footnotes

[1] James Hallas, *The Devil's Anvil: The Assault on Peleliu*, Westport, Connecticut: Praeger Publishers, 1994, p. 255.

[2] Bill Raynor, E-mail to author, 28 March 2004.

[3] David Hinchley, E-mail to author, 30 April 2004.

[4] David Hinchley, E-mail to author, 30 April 2004.

[5] Corydon Wagner, "The Bones of Nakagawa," *Naval History*. Washington, D.C.: United States Naval Institute, February 2003.

[6] Mike Dunn, "Tracing Scars, Ghosts of War," *Tampa Tribune* (Metro Section), May 30, 2004, pp. 1,10.

[7] Bob Hope, "A century of Hope - Bob Hope's life and career," *Saturday Evening Post*, July-August, 1998.

[8] Landing Ship Transport (LST) for the transport and deployment of troops, vehicles, tanks and supplies.

Interview with Everett Pope

August 4, 2002

Everett Pope was born in Milton, Massachusetts on July 16, 1919. He was Phi Beta Kappa at Bowdoin College in Maine. He was discharged from the Marines after the war at the rank of Major. He was awarded the Medal of Honor "for conspicuous gallantry and intrepidity at the risk of his life above and beyond the call of duty while serving as Commanding Officer of Company C, First Battalion, First Marines, First Marine Division, during action against enemy Japanese forces on Peleliu Island, Palau Group, on 19-20 September 1944."[1]

Although the combined company strength was 400 men, Pope's original "C" Company consisted of 235 men. Casualties had reduced the unit to 90, and 24 made it to the top of Hill 100, only to realize that they had no support behind them and were surrounded by enemy soldiers. They were attacked in waves resulting in fierce fighting throughout the night. Pope and his men had little ammunition, and resorted to lobbing Japanese grenades back and engaged in hand-to-hand combat, sometimes tossing attacking enemy off the cliffs, and throwing rocks in desperation.

Only eight were left when they fought their way back down the next morning. Pope's radioman was killed by machine-gun fire as Pope was talking on the radio next to him. Pope knew he needed artillery support, but he also knew more men would have been killed in "friendly fire." Later during the battle, he received orders to take back a ridge that was lost when he and his men were ordered down from the hill. He didn't have enough men left, and the order was rescinded. Pope was the only commander to hold his post throughout the battle.[2]

The 1st Marine Division commander was Major General William H. Rupertus. Pope's commanding officer was Colonel Lewis B. "Chesty" Puller. Company commander Pope has commented upon the "straight ahead" attack method. His company was asked to make repeated assaults against the Umurbrogol. He said, "Why he wanted me and my men dead on top of that hill, I don't know. Don't know what purpose it would have served."[3]

This is a transcript of a personal interview with him. Pope was extremely cordial, and you can hear the New Englander in his voice. He repeatedly asked me to pay his respects to my father, as Pope knows more than anyone what it was like for the USMC fighting men in the Peleliu battle, noting that it was unnecessary for so many to lose their lives because of faulty intelligence, and, in the final analysis, there was little strategic advantage.

P. M. Finelli: Thank you for returning my telephone call yesterday evening. I'm sorry I wasn't here to receive it. I hope I am not interrupting you, but I would like to speak with you if it is convenient. I was able to contact you through the efforts of my sister Chris, who lives in Massachusetts and read Kevin Rothstein's interview in the Patriot Ledger, October 25th of last year, and obtained your telephone number from him.

Everett Pope: Oh yes, I remember that.

PMF: My father was a Marine Corps combat veteran wounded on Peleliu by a Japanese bayonet. I spoke with him about Peleliu in New England in June, and my family has asked me to create a narrative record of his WWII experiences.

Pope: Is your father still alive?

PMF: Yes, he and my mother are alive and well. They have been married since 1948.

Pope: That's very good. I'm glad to hear that.

PMF: Anyone who researches the battle for Peleliu soon discovers that virtually every historical account includes what you and your men did to win that ground known as Hill 100, or Walt's Ridge, now known as Pope Hill, or Pope's Ridge.

Pope: We're trying to go back to calling it Hill 100 again.

PMF: One book, *The Devil's Anvil* written by James Hallas, says that you were the only company commander in the 1st Battalion to retain his post throughout the entire operation. McMillan's book *The Old Breed* also has an extraordinary account of what happened up there.

Pope: There have been many other books about the battle, and Hallas's is one of the best in my opinion.

PMF: I have the utmost respect for what you and your men did to win that ground, and hold it throughout the night despite impossible odds. It is a remarkable story of heroism and extraordinary courage under fire, defending indefensible territory through courage, guts and steadfast commitment to duty. In order to help better understand what happened during that battle, I wonder if I might ask a few questions. If you'd like, I could tell you more about my Dad's experience, but I'm primarily interested in your perspective in my attempt to understand the Peleliu battle.

Pope: What was your father's unit?

PMF: He had a temporary pre-invasion assignment with the UDT-6 beach recon team from September 1 until the 16th, when he was re-assigned to the 3rd Battalion, 1st Marines, "K" Company on Umurbrogol to clean caves, pill boxes, mines and duds. On the 21st he spent another five days supporting 2nd Battalion, 7th Marines, "K" Company. He was wounded by Japanese bayonet in hand-to-hand combat on the 26th of September while sealing caves with satchel charges and Bangalore torpedoes on Bloody Nose Ridge.

Pope: Please give my deepest respects to your father. It has been very difficult for many of us who have lived happy lives since then, but cannot forget what happened back then.

PMF: Thank you, I will convey your words to him. Evidently the Navy, under Admiral Jesse B. Oldendorf, shelled the beach for a couple of days on the 12th and 13th, supposedly "softening up" the enemy. He claimed they had run out of targets, but an area called "The Point" was never targeted, and many ships left for the Philippines. What was your impression of the effectiveness of that pre-invasion shelling on the enemy's defenses when you and your unit went into battle?

Pope: I have a very low opinion of the effectiveness of the Navy's bombardment. They did a bad job, practically useless. The enemy was entrenched in the protective cover of jungle and had reinforced cannon and machine guns in stone bunkers in the hills and mountains.

PMF: Where exactly was Hill 100 in relation to Umurbrogol?

Pope: It was at the extreme right of Umurbrogol as you look at the battle map and we saw no effect of the shelling in that area at all.

PMF: Could you tell me about your own unit's pre-invasion preparation and briefings? What did you know about what to expect once you landed on the beach?

Pope: As Marines, we were well prepared in the combat sense. We were trained for battle and ready to fight. The failure was with intelligence, and the briefings were incorrect. We were told it would be a walk-through with little resistance. It was quite the opposite.

PMF: Were you aware of any Marines involved in pre-invasion beach re-con in the water with the UDT units?

Pope: Not at the time, but we learned later that Marines had taken part in the beach reconnaissance with the UDT Teams.

PMF: My father was in the water for three days, between September 12ᵗʰ and 14ᵗʰ. He kept a journal in which he relates that on the 14ᵗʰ there were anti-ship mines laced to horned scullies and coral cairns set out about 100 yards from the beach. Some of them were not armed, the safety pin wasn't pulled and they were not there the day before. He said that the Japanese had to have their own swimmers. Amazingly, they had also buried some aircraft bombs in the beach with pressure fuses. They also found fuel drums laced to the fringing coral. He said the Japanese had to work like hell to get that done so quickly.

Pope: The Japanese had done a lot to make our landing difficult. As it turned out, Peleliu was heavily defended by the enemy. We took the island with heavy casualties. After all, the battle wasn't necessary in a strategic sense.

PMF: MacArthur was already on his way to Leyte where he landed in October 1944.

Pope: Yes. We didn't have to take Peleliu, but we did what we were asked to do.

PMF: Did you retire from the Marine Corps?

Pope: Oh no, I was discharged at the rank of Major, put down my sword and went home.

PMF: I'm sure you are asked for interviews about Peleliu quite often. This is a personal question, but it has a lot to do with how brave men like you have handled those horrific combat experiences. What has it been like for you after all of these years, and how do you handle those feelings and memories?

Pope: I have had a happy and satisfying life. We did what needed to be done during the war. I have no regrets, no sense of recrimination. I sometimes question the tactics. Mrs. Pope and I went back to Peleliu for the 50ᵗʰ anniversary of the invasion to pay our respects. We shed a tear or two and remembered those men who lost their lives. The island has changed. It was denuded during the battle and the vegetation has grown back. Now it is a prime destination for scuba divers. As a matter of fact, I'm watching television right now wearing a T-shirt someone sent me from Peleliu. It mentions a paradise for scuba divers, but nothing about the battle. There is a small village there now. There were no villages on the island in 1944. The people do things like fishing, growing small crops, including marijuana, and tourists come and visit to see and explore the battle sites. It is now part of the Republic of Palau.

PMF: My uncle, who was an Air Force pilot, is the only other one in our family who has seen the island, having flown over it many years ago on his way to Vietnam. I would like to visit and see the island where my father served and was wounded in combat.

Pope: When you go, give me a call and I will give you some names of people on the island. They can help you.

PMF: Thank you so much for taking the time to talk about Peleliu with me.

Pope: You are welcome. Please don't forget to give my respects to your father.

Footnotes
[1] Please refer to appendix C for Captain Pope's complete Medal of Honor citation.
[2] There is more information on Hill 100 in George McMillan's article, *The Old Breed*, Infantry Journal Press, 1949.
[3] Jon T. Hoffman, "The Truth About Peleliu," Annapolis, MD: United States Naval Institute, *Proceedings*, Nov 2002, Vol. 128, Iss. 11, p. 53.

B

Command and Staff[1]

Expeditionary Troops

Commanding General: Maj. Gen. Julian C. Smith
Chief of Staff: Col. Dudley S. Brown

III Amphibious Corps

Commanding General: Maj. Gen. Roy S. Geiger
Chief of Staff: Col. Merwin H. Silverthorn

1st Marine Division

Commanding General: Maj. Gen. William H. Rupertus
Assistant Division Commander: Brig. Gen. Oliver P. Smith
Chief of Staff: Col. John T. Selden

Division Headquarters Battalion

Commanding Officer: Col. Joseph F. Hankins (KIA 3 Oct. 1944)
Commanding Officer: Lt. Col. Austin C. Shofner (from 3 Oct)

1st Pioneer Battalion

Commanding Officer: Lt. Col. Robert G. Balance
Executive Officer: Maj. Nathaniel Morgenthal

1st Marines

Commanding Officer: Col. Lewis B. Puller
Executive Officer: Lt. Col. Richard P. Ross, Jr.

1st Bn, 1st Marines

Commanding Officer: Maj. Raymond G. Davis
Executive Officer: Maj. Nikolai S. Stevenson

Commander, "C" Company: Captain Everett P. Pope

2nd Bn, 1st Marines

Commanding Officer: Lt. Col. Russell E. Honsowetz
Executive Officer: Maj. Charles H. Brush, Jr.

3rd Bn, 1st Marines

Commanding Officer: Lt. Col. Stephen V. Sabol
Executive Officer: Maj. William McNulty

Commander, "K" Company: George P. Hunt

5th Marines

Commanding Officer: Col. Harold D. Harris
Executive Officer: Lt. Col. Lewis W. Walt

1st Bn, 5th Marines

Commanding Officer: Lt. Col. Robert W. Boyd
Executive Officer: Maj. Harold T. A. Richmond

2nd Bn, 5th Marines

Commanding Officer: Maj. Gordon D. Gayle
Executive Officer: Maj. John H. Gustafson

3rd Bn, 5th Marines

Commanding Officer: Lt. Col. Austin C. Shofner (to 15 Sept.)
Commanding Officer: Lt. Col. Lewis W. Walt (15/16 Sept.)
Commanding Officer: Maj. John H. Gustafson (from 16 Sept.)

Executive Officer: Maj. Robert M. Ash (to 15 Sept.)
Executive Officer: Maj. Hierome L. Opie (from 16 Sept.)

7th Marines

Commanding Officer: Col. Herman H. Hanneken
Executive Officer: Lt. Col. Norman Hussa

1st Bn, 7th Marines

Commanding Officer: Lt. Col. John J. Gormely
Executive Officer: Maj. Waite W. Worden

2nd Bn, 7th Marines

Commanding Officer: Lt. Col. Spencer S. Berger
Executive Officer: Maj. Elbert D. Graves (to 20 Sept.)
Executive Officer: Maj. John F. Weber (from 21 Sept.)

3rd Bn, 7th Marines

Commanding Officer: Maj. E. Hunter Hurst
Executive Officer: Maj. Victor H. Streit

11th Marines

Commanding Officer: Col. William H. Harrison
Executive Officer: Lt. Col. Edson L. Lyman

1st Bn, 11th Marines

Commanding Officer: Lt. Col. Richard W. Wallace
Executive Officer: Maj. James H. Moffatt, Jr.

2nd Bn, 11th Marines

Commanding Officer: Lt. Col. Noah P. Wood, Jr.
Executive Officer: Maj. Floyd C. Maner (to 15 Sept.)
Executive Officer: Maj. John P. McAllin (from 16 Sept.)

3rd Bn, 11th Marines

Commanding Officer: Lt. Col. Charles M. Nees
Executive Officer: Maj. William J. Hannan

4th Bn, 11th Marines

Commanding Officer: Lt. Col. Luis C. Reinberg
Executive Officer: Maj. George E. Bowdoin

Footnotes

[1] Frank Hough, *The Assault on Peleliu*, Washington, DC: Historical Division Headquarters, USMC, 1950, pp. 205-209.

Medal of Honor Citations
The Battle of Peleliu

Medal of Honor Plaque on Peleliu Marine Memorial
GPS Coordinates: N 07° 00.645'; E 134° 14.165'
(Photo © 2004 Patrick Finelli)

CORPORAL LEWIS K. BAUSELL
UNITED STATES MARINE CORPS

"For conspicuous gallantry and intrepidity at the risk of his life above and beyond the call of duty while serving with the First Battalion, Fifth Marines, First Marine Division, during action against enemy Japanese forces on Peleliu Island, Palau Group, 15 September 1944. Valiantly placing himself at the head of his squad, Corporal Bausell led the charge forward against a hostile pillbox which was covering a vital sector of the beach and, as the first to reach the emplacement, immediately started firing his automatic into the aperture while the remainder of his men closed in on the enemy. Swift to act a Japanese grenade was hurled into their midst, Corporal Bausell threw himself on the deadly weapon, taking the full blast of the explosion and sacrificing his own life to save his men. His unwavering loyalty and inspiring courage reflect the highest credit upon Corporal Bausell and the United States Naval Service. He gallantly gave his life for his country."

Franklin D. Roosevelt
President of the United States

PRIVATE FIRST CLASS ARTHUR J. JACKSON
UNITED STATES MARINE CORPS

"For conspicuous gallantry and intrepidity at the risk of his life above and beyond the call of duty while serving with the Third Battalion, Seventh Marines, First Marine Division, in action against enemy Japanese forces on the Island of Peleliu in the Palau Group, 18 September 1944. Boldly taking the initiative when his platoon's left flank advance was held up by the fire of Japanese troops concealed in strong fortified positions, Private First Class Jackson unhesitatingly proceeded forward of our lines and, courageously defying the heavy barrages, charged a large pillbox housing approximately thirty-five enemy soldiers. Pouring his automatic fire into the opening of the fixed installation to trap the occupying troops, he hurled white phosphorus grenades and explosive charges brought up by a fellow Marine, demolishing the pillbox and killing all of the enemy. Advancing alone under the continuous fire from other hostile emplacements, he employed a similar means to smash two smaller positions in the immediate vicinity. Determined to crush the entire pocket of resistance although harassed on all sides by the shattering blasts of Japanese weapons and covered only by small rifle parties, he stormed one gun position after another, dealing death and destruction to

166

the savagely fighting enemy in his inexorable drive against the remaining defenses and succeeded in wiping out a total of twelve pillboxes and fifty Japanese soldiers. Stouthearted and indomitable despite the terrific odds, Private First Class Jackson resolutely maintained control of the platoon's left flank movement throughout his valiant one-man assault and, by his cool decision and relentless fighting spirit during a critical situation, contributed essentially to the complete annihilation of the enemy in the southern sector of the island. His gallant initiative and heroic conduct in the face of extreme peril reflect the highest credit upon Private First Class Jackson and the United States Naval Service."

Harry S. Truman
President of the United States

PRIVATE FIRST CLASS RICHARD E. KRAUS
UNITED STATES MARINE CORPS RESERVE

"For conspicuous gallantry and intrepidity at the risk of his life above and beyond the call of duty while serving with the Eighth Amphibian Tractor Battalion, Third Amphibious Corps, Fleet Marine Force, in action against enemy Japanese forces on Peleliu, Palau Islands, on 3 October 1944. Unhesitatingly volunteering for the extremely hazardous mission of evacuating a wounded comrade from the front lines, Private First Class Kraus and three companions courageously made their way forward and successfully penetrated the lines for some distance before the enemy opened with an intense, devastating barrage of hand grenades which forced the stretcher party to take cover and subsequently abandon the mission. While returning to the rear, they observed two men approaching who appeared to be Marines and immediately demanded the password. When instead of answering, one of the two Japanese threw a hand grenade into the midst of the group, Private First Class Kraus heroically flung himself upon the grenade and, covering it with his body, absorbed the full impact of the explosion and was instantly killed. By his prompt action and great personal valor in the face of almost certain death, he saved the lives of his three companions, and his loyal spirit of self-sacrifice reflects the highest credit upon himself and the United States Naval Service. He gallantly gave his life for his comrades."

Harry S. Truman
President of the United States

PRIVATE FIRST CLASS JOHN D. NEW
UNITED STATES MARINE CORPS

"For conspicuous gallantry and intrepidity at the risk of his own life above and beyond the call of duty while serving with the Second Battalion, Seventh Marines, First Marine Division, in action against enemy Japanese forces on Peleliu Island, Palau Group, 25 September 1944. When a Japanese soldier emerged from a cave in a cliff directly below an observation post and suddenly hurled a grenade into the position from which two of our men were directing mortar fire against enemy emplacements, Private First Class New instantly perceived the dire peril to the other Marines and, with utter disregard for his own safety, unhesitatingly flung himself upon the grenade and absorbed the full impact of the explosion, thus saving the lives of the two observers. Private First Class New's great personal valor and selfless conduct in the face of almost certain death reflect the highest credit upon himself and the United States Naval Service. He gallantly gave his life for his country."

Franklin D. Roosevelt
President of the United States

PRIVATE FIRST CLASS WESLEY PHELPS
UNITED STATES MARINE CORPS RESERVE

"For conspicuous gallantry and intrepidity at the risk of his life above and beyond the call of duty while serving with the Third Battalion, Seventh Marines, First Marine Division, in action against enemy Japanese forces on Peleliu Island, Palau Group, during a savage hostile counterattack on the night of 4 October

1944. Stationed with another Marine in an advanced position when a Japanese hand grenade landed in his foxhole, Private First Class Phelps instantly shouted a warning to his comrade and rolled over on the deadly bomb, absorbing with his own body the full, shattering impact of the exploding charge. Courageous and indomitable, Private First Class Phelps fearlessly gave his life that another might be spared serious injury and his great valor and heroic devotion to duty in the face of certain death reflected the highest credit upon himself and the United States Naval Service. He gallantly gave his life for his country."

Harry S. Truman
President of the United States

CAPTAIN EVERETT P. POPE
UNITED STATES MARINE CORPS

"For conspicuous gallantry and intrepidity at the risk of his life above and beyond the call of duty while serving as Commanding Officer of Company C, First Battalion, First Marines, First Marine Division, during action against enemy Japanese forces on Peleliu Island, Palau Group, on 19-20 September 1944. Subjected to point-blank cannon fire, which caused heavy casualties and badly disorganized his company while assaulting a steep coral hill, Captain Pope rallied his men and gallantly led them to the summit in the face of machine-gun, mortar, and sniper fire. Forced by wide spread hostile attack to deploy the remnants of his company thinly in order to hold the ground won, and with his machine-guns out of action and insufficient water and ammunition, he remained on the exposed hill with twelve men and one wounded officer, determined to hold through the night. Attacked continuously with grenades, machine-guns, and rifles from three sides and twice subjected to suicidal charges during the night, he and his valiant men fiercely beat back or destroyed the enemy, resorting to hand-to-hand combat as the supply of ammunition dwindled and still maintaining his lines with his eight remaining riflemen when daylight brought more deadly fire and he was ordered to withdraw.

His valiant leadership against devastating odds while protecting the units below from heavy Japanese attack reflects the highest credit upon Captain Pope and the United States Naval Service."

Franklin D. Roosevelt
President of the United States

PRIVATE FIRST CLASS CHARLES H. ROAN
UNITED STATES MARINE CORPS RESERVE

"For conspicuous gallantry and intrepidity at the risk of his life above and beyond the call of duty while serving with the Second Battalion, Seventh Marines, First Marine Division, in action against enemy Japanese Forces on Peleliu, Palau Islands, 18 September 1944. Shortly after his leader ordered a withdrawal upon discovering the squad was partly cut off from their company as a result of their rapid advance along an exposed ridge during an aggressive attack on the strongly entrenched enemy, Private First Class Roan and his companions were suddenly engaged in a furious exchange of hand grenades with Japanese forces emplaced in a cave on higher ground and the rear of the squad. Seeking protection with four other Marines in a depression in the rocky, broken terrain, Private First Class Roan was wounded by an enemy grenade which fell close to their position and, immediately realizing the imminent peril to his comrades when another grenade landed in the midst of the group, unhesitatingly flung himself upon it, covering it with his body and absorbing the full impact of the explosion. By his prompt action and selfless conduct in the face of almost certain death, he saved the lives of four men. His great personal valor reflects the highest credit upon himself and the United States Naval Service. He gallantly gave his life for his comrades."

Harry S. Truman
President of the United States

FIRST LIEUTENANT CARLTON R. ROUH
UNITED STATES MARINE CORPS RESERVE

"For conspicuous gallantry and intrepidity at the risk of his life above and beyond the call of duty while attached to the First Battalion, Fifth Marines, First Marine Division, during action against enemy Japanese forces on Peleliu Island, Palau Group, 15 September 1944. Before permitting his men to use an enemy dugout as a position for an 81-mm mortar observation post, First Lieutenant Rouh made a personal reconnaissance of the pillbox and, upon entering, was severely wounded by Japanese rifle fire from within. Emerging from the dugout, he was immediately assisted by two Marines to a less exposed area, but while receiving first aid, was further endangered by an enemy grenade which was thrown into their midst. Quick to act in spite of his weakened condition, he lurched to a crouching position and thrust both men aside, placing his own body between them and the grenade and taking the full blast of the explosion himself. His exceptional spirit of loyalty and self-sacrifice in the face of almost certain death reflects the highest credit upon First Lieutenant Rouh and the United States Naval Service."

Franklin D. Roosevelt
President of the United States

D

Presidential Unit Citation

The President of the United States takes pleasure in presenting the
PRESIDENTIAL UNIT CITATION to the

FIRST MARINE DIVISION (REINFORCED)

consisting of FIRST Marine Division; First Amphibian Tractor Battalion, FMF; U. S. Navy Flame Thrower Unit Attached; Sixth Amphibian Tractor Battalion (Provisional), FMF; Third Armored Amphibian Battalion (Provisional), FMF; Detachment Eighth Amphibian Tractor Battalion, FMF; 454th Amphibian Truck Company, U. S. Army; 456th Amphibian Truck Company, U. S. Army; Fourth Joint Assault Signal Company, FMF; Fifth Separate Wire Platoon, FMF; Sixth Separate Wire Platoon, FMF,

for service as set forth in the following

CITATION:

"For extraordinary heroism in action against enemy Japanese forces at Peleliu and Ngesebus from September 15 to 29, 1944. Landing over a treacherous coral reef against hostile mortar and artillery fire, the FIRST Marine Division, Reinforced, seized a narrow, heavily mined beachhead and advanced foot by foot in the face of relentless enfilade fire through rainforests and mangrove swamps toward the air strip, the key to the enemy defenses of the southern Palaus. Opposed all the way by thoroughly disciplined, veteran Japanese troops heavily entrenched in caves and in reinforced concrete pillboxes which honeycombed the high ground throughout the island, the officers and men of the Division fought with undiminished spirit and courage despite heavy losses, exhausting heat and difficult terrain, seizing and holding a highly strategic air and land base for future operations in the Western Pacific. By their individual acts of heroism, their aggressiveness and their fortitude, the men of the FIRST Marine Division, Reinforced, upheld the highest traditions of the United States Naval Service."

For the President,

Frank Knox

Secretary of the Navy

appendix

E

Explanation of Japanese Plan for Chichi Jima

These pages contain scans of an original document typed by
Major Yoshitaka Horie, Japanese officer in charge at Chichi Jima,
the central base of supply and communication between Japan and
the Bonin Islands. Major Horie, staff to Lt. Gen. Todamichi
Kuribayashi, was responsible for control of arms and supply traffic
to Iwo Jima. He was Iwo's "Emergency Supply Officer." The
Major would survive the campaign to become its chief Japanese
chronicler. Thanks to him, the world knows more of the Japanese
side of the Iwo battle than any of the other island battles. The
document was written by Major Horie on December 23, 1945 and
kept by my uncle, a U. S. Navy Radarman on LST 871. His vessel
went to Chichi Jima with five wooden minesweepers to clear the
minefields and channels. U. S. forces occupied those islands after
the war. The meetings with Major Horie were held on his ship.

March 23, 1945 was the last day that Kuribayashi's radioman
got through to Major Horie's relay station on Chichi Jima. At about
5 o'clock the station received the message "All officers and men
of Chichi Jima, good bye. A weeping Horie ordered the radioman
to stand by, just in case something further came through. But there
were no more messages from Iwo Jima. Ah!"[1] Major Horie's
report mentions Col. Presley M. Rixey, USMC, Commander of
the Bonin's Occupation Force.[2] The Chichi Marines served as the
occupation force for the Bonin Islands. My father shared copies
of the original Japanese Defense Plan documents with the "Chichi
Marines" at their reunion in 2003. The late Sergeant Louis R.
Lowery took pictures in the Bonins and on Chichi Jima while
serving as a photographer for *Leatherneck*. Major Horie supplied
other photographs from Japan, including portraits of Kuribayashi
secured from the general's widow. The Marine Historical Division

has archived many of the images. After communication ceased a few years ago, the last reports indicated that Major Horie was suffering from Alzheimer's disease.

Major Yoshitaka Horie
(Courtesy of Marine Historical Division. Reprinted in Wheeler, p. 59.)

Major Horie reports that after Iwo Jima, the U. S. forces went to Okinawa and did not bother with the Bonin Islands. Horie had the maps and offered to share his knowledge of the Japanese defense plan, a strategy based not on the possibility of victory, but on inflicting the maximum number of casualties on American fighting men (estimated at 150,000). He indicates in the document that the decisive blow to Japan was the result of American "greatness of mass-production, superior technique, skillful movement and especially pre-eminence of joint operation."[3] My uncle sent these historic documents to my father in 1992.

Major Horie interrogated four of the eight American "Flyboys" shot down during bombing raids on Chichi Jima.[4] According to James Bradley, "Floyd Hall gave Horie English lessons in his office."[5] He tried to protect the other American flyers but, unfortunately, he could not save their lives. The Battle of Iwo Jima took place in February 1945 at approximately the same time the pilots were brutalized as prisoners on Chichi. In 1947, Major Horie testified against the Japanese officers who committed atrocities upon the eight "Chichi Flyboys."[6]

A submarine rescued a ninth pilot from the waters of Chichi Jima, former President George H. W. Bush. He was shot down as a Navy flyer on September 2, 1944. Two members of his flight crew perished.

The novelist Jack London (*Call of the Wild, White Fang*) wrote a monograph in 1895 while at Oakland High School (*Bonin Islands: An Incident of the Sealing Fleet of '93*). The British established an outpost there in 1830. Commodore Matthew Perry arrived in 1853 and bought some land for $50 from an American. Chichi Jima was the first territory in the Eastern Pacific to come under the jurisdiction of the United States. There has been a gradual decline in descendants of mutineers, adventurers and swashbucklers from the 19th century as Japanese culture predominates.

Footnotes

[1] Richard Wheeler, *A Special Valor, The Marines and the Pacific War*, pp. 331, 333, 404. Wheeler credits Maj. Horie in his Preface, and quotes him on pages 13-30, 204, 210-211.

[2] Robert Sherrod, *History of Marine Corps Aviation in World War II*, Baltimore, Maryland : The Nautical & Aviation Publishing Company of America, pp. 350-356.

[3] Japanese Defense Plan. Original document.

[4] James Bradley, *Flyboys*, Boston: Little, Brown and Company, 2003, p. 209-210.

[5] James Bradley, *Flyboys*, Boston: Little, Brown and Company, 2003, p. 256.

[6] James Bradley. *Flyboys*. Boston: Little, Brown and Company, 2003, pp. 209, 210.

Explanation

of

Japanese Defence Plan of Chichi Jima

December 23, 1945

Y. HORIE

Major

EXPLANATION
OF
JAPANESE DEFENCE PLAN OF CHICHI JIMA

DECEMBER 23, 1945

Contents

1. Preface.

2. General Situation.

    a. History of Bonin Islands.

    b. Situation of Spring, 1944.

    c. Situation of Summer, 1944.

    d. Situation of January, 1945.

3. Defence of Chichi Jima.

    a. My judgment regarding anti enemy's plan.

    b. My judgment in connection with American Strength and
       landing direction, when American Forces will assault
       Chichi Jima.

    c. My premise regarding defence plan of Chichi Jima.

    d. Approximate number of Our Strength, Arms and Ammunitions.
       (Army and Navy).

    e. Special character of my defence plan.

    f. Details of defence.

4. Conclusion.

1. Preface

It is indeed a great honour for me to have this golden opportunity of expressing my humble opinion regarding defense plan of Chichi Jima in the presence of many American Officers. My English is very poor and I am sure you will find many difficulties in my talk. But as I should like to express what I have in my mind thoroughly I venture to make my speech in English.

I should like to have your permission for my discourtesy.

2. General Situation

    a. History of Bonin Islands

About seventy years ago Bonin Islands became the territory of Japan. In connection with this history, Colonel RIXEY knows better than I do, so I will not touch it. At 1914, just when the World War No. I occured, General of the Army Y. UEHARA, Chief of the General Staff, insisted on the importance of fortifying Chichi Jima and Amami Oshima for national defense, and began to make fortress at Chichi and after several years he placed one part of the heavy artillery.

But as a result of the Washington Conference, we were obliged to stop the reinforcement of this fortress and at the beginning of the World War No. II we had only Fortress headquarters, 24 cm howitzer 4, 15 cm cannon 2 and 12 cm howitzer 2 in Army.

On the other hand, in Navy, we constructed the radio station at 1937, made the Air Force at 1942, and at 1943 Naval Base Headquarters.

    b. Situation of Spring, 1944.

"Truck" was raided by American task force at February and Palau at March 1944.

On that time our strength of Sea and Air forces became about half of that of America. Therefore Japanese Imperial Headquarters made the Central Pacific Fleet Headquarters (Commander in Chief was Vice Admiral T. NAGUMO) and the 31st Army Headquarters (Commander was Lieutenant General E. OBATA) at Saipan and endeavored to reinforce the Army and Navy of the Middle Pacific area thoroughly.

Our strength of Bonin Islands at March were as follows:

	Imo	Chichi	Muko	Haha
Army	3,000	3,000	500	1,000
Navy	2,000	2,000	20	500

The Commander of the 31st Army instructed the Commander of Chichi Jima fortress to bring Army and Navy of Bonin Islands under single control.

    c. Situation of Summer, 1944.

From March to June Japanese Imperail Headquarters have sent about ten divisions to Middle Pacific area and specially did their very best to strengthen Saipan, Guam and palau, and on the other hand endeavored to reestablish our Great Fleet.

In those days, at Tokyo, we were discussing many times regarding the value of Iwo Jima.

Since we had the first air raid on Bonin Island from American Air Forces on 15th of June, their air raids became severer each time.

When American forces landed on Saipan on 15th of June, Japanese Imperial Headquarters planned to send our Great Fleet (They were south of the Philippines) to Saipan and give decisive blow to t he American Pacific Fleet, and let our 5th Fleet and about two divisions repossess Saipan.

On that time I was at Tokyo being appointed as a staff
officer of the 31st Army and went on board with the first group
of this repossessing forces under the command of the 5th Fleet.

But on 19th of June our Great Fleet was completely
defeated by your 5th Fleet at 270 miles north of Yap Island and
lost nearly all of the carrier planes. Then Japanese Imperial
Headquarters gave up their plan of repossessing Saipan, stopped
the dispatch of the 5th Fleet and determined to reinforce the
Bonin Islands with this first group and some other units.

On 30th of June the 109th Divisional Headquarters was
made at Iwo appointing Lieutenant General KURIBAYASHI as the
Divisional Commander and I became a staff officer of this Division.

Situation of Bonin Islands at 30th of June was as follows:

Army: Army was direct under Japanese Imperial
Headquarters. Lieutenant General KURIBAYASHI placed his forces
as follows:

At Iwo — Main power of Divisional headquarters 2nd mixed
         brigade and other troops.

At Chichi — 1st mixed brigade and other troops under the
(Ani, Muko) command of Colonel MASAKI.

At Chichi Jima was the only central base of supply and
communication between Japan and Bonin Islands. Lieutenant General
KURIBAYASHI placed here the dispatched headquarters as Major HORIE
the head of it.

I was ordered to supply materials to each island,
communicate with Tokyo and each island.

Navy. At Iwo we had the 27th Air Force under the command of
the 3rd Air Fleet newly constructed Kisarazu. Commander of
Chichi Jima Naval Base placed Navy of Chichi and Haha under his
single control, and he was under the command of Yokosuka Admiralty
Port.

    d. Situation of January, 1945.

      Strength of Bonin Islands were as follows:

	Iwo	Chichi	Ani	Muko	Haha
Army	17,500	8,000	350	600	3,500
Navy	5,500	6,000			3,000

3. Defense of Chichi Jima.

    a. My judgement regarding anti enemy's plan.

Until American forces landed on Iwo I thought American
forces will assault Iwo and Chichi or Haha at the same time.

When American forces occupied Iwo and went to Okinawa I
felt that Chichi may be by-passed.

But in order to provide against your sudden attack and for
my honour I did my best to make this fortress much stronger.

    b. My judgement in connection with American strength and
landing direction, when American forces will assault Chichi Jima.

-2-

```
                                          (Comparison with the
                                           Japanese Division)
          Land forces   Army or Marine Division  3      (3)
          Sea forces    Battle Ship              6     (30)
                        Cruiser                 15     (15)
                        Destroyer               40     ( 8)
          Air Forces    Airplanes             3000     (43)
              Total                      (about 100)
```

In connection with the landing direction I will explain on the sand model.

   c. My premise regarding Defense Plan of Chichi Jima we did not have any fleet, air force, supply and reinforcement.

   d. Approximate number of our strength, arms and ammunitions (Army and Navy).

```
          Officers and men                        15,000
          Arms (and ammunitions) Big guns 160,     50,000
                                 Small guns 15,000  9,000,000
          Torpedo and Suicide boats                   150
```

   e. Special character of my Defense Plan.

      (a) Complete fortification (After three years we were
           able to connect each position with gallery).
      (b) Make depth position from beach to the top of the
           mountains.
      (c) No offensive operation at the seaside.
      (d) No reserve.
      (e) Attach importance on sniping.
      (f) Use anti-aircraft gun as artillery.

   f. My estimate of Enemy's loss and our fighting term.

      (a) Estimate of Enemy's loss:
```
                                   (The dead)
           By big guns          50,000(One man - one round)
           By small guns        90,000(One man - 100 rounds)
           By hand shell        10,000(    "     "      )
           By suicide boats and other
                    Total      150,000
```

      (b) Fighting term

           About three months.

   g. Details of defense.

           Refer to my booklet.

4. Conclusion

   What gave decisive blow to Japan in the World War No II were American submarines and Air forces. Japan lost most of her Navy and transport by the American submarines and Air forces.

   I pay my respects to your greatness of mass-production, superior technique, skillfull movement and especially pre-eminence of joint operation. I experienced bitterly how difficult it is to defend the island when there are no fleet, no air forces and no supply coming. Even though our death and fall of this island was evident we were to continue our fighting to the last and give tremendous damage to the enemy. For this purpose we need perservering spirit. I did my best to fight for the honour, reminding Lieutenant General Gondler CHINCO of Russia who was in charge of the defense of Port Arthur 45 years ago. Last of all I thank you very much for your kind attention to my humble speech.

Bibliography

Bailey, Dan E.. *World War II Wrecks of Palau*. Redding, California: North Valley Diver Publications, 2000.

Bailey, Dan E. *World War II Wrecks of the Truk Lagoon*. Redding, California: North Valley Diver Publications, 2000.

Blassingame, Wyatt. *The U.S. Frogmen of World War II*. New York: Random House, 1964.

Bradley, James. *Flyboys*. Boston: Little, Brown and Company, 2003.

Cunningham, Chet. *Hell Wouldn't Stop*. New York: Carroll & Graf, 2002.

Dunn, Mike. "Tracing Scars, Ghosts of War." *Tampa Tribune*. May 30, 2004 (Metro Section): 1,10.

Eyerman, J. R. "Palau: Huge U.S. Task Force Sails to Western Edge of Pacific to Pound Japanese Base." *Life* v16n17 (April 24, 1944): 34-35.

Falk, Stanley. *Palaus: Bloodiest Victory*. New York: Ballantine, 1974.

Fane, Francis. Letter to Patrick L. Finelli. 1 March 1988.

Fane, Francis. *The Naked Warriors: The Elite Fighting Force That Became The Navy Seals*. New York: Appleton Century-Croft, Inc., 1956.

Fee, James. *The Peleliu Project*. Philadelphia: Seraphim Gallery, 2002.

Finelli, Patrick L. Personal interview. 17 June 2002.

Flynn, W. T. "Letters to UDT 7-WWII." *Fire in the Hole*. UDT-SEAL Museum Association. Summer 2004.

Gailey, Harry. *Peleliu: 1944*. Baltimore: The Nautical & Aviation Publishing Company of America, 1983.

Gayle, Gordon D. *Bloody Beaches: The Marines at Peleliu*. Washington, DC: Marine Corps Historical Center, 1996.

Gayle, Gordon D. Letter to Patrick M. Finelli. 6 August 2004.

Gilliland, Ann Owens. *Peleliu Remembered*. Peleliu Museum Monograph, 2002.

Hallas, James H. *The Devil's Anvil: Assault on Peleliu*. Westport, Connecticut: Praeger Publishers, 1994.

Hanauer, Eric. *Diving Micronesia*. Locust Valley, New York: Aqua Quest Publications, 2001.

Hinchley, David. E-mail to author. 30 April 2004.

Hoffman, Jon T. "The Truth About Peleliu." *Proceedings*. Washington, D.C.: United States Naval Institute, November 2002.

Hope, Bob and Martin, Pete. "A century of Hope - Bob Hope's life and career." *Saturday Evening Post*. July-August, 1998.

Hough, Frank. *The Assault on Peleliu*. Washington, DC: Historical Division Headquarters, USMC, 1950.

Hunt, George P. *Coral Comes High*. The Battery Press, 1946.

Isely, Jeter A. and Crowl, Philip. *The U.S. Marines and Amphibious War*. Princeton: Princeton University Press, 1951.

Lane, Kerry. *Marine Pioneers: The Unsung Heroes of World War II*. Atglen, Pennsylvania: Schiffer Military/Aviation History. 1997.

Lea, Tom. *Battle Stations: A Grizzly from the Coral Sea, Peleliu Landing*. El Paso: Hertzog, 1945.

Lea, Tom. "Peleliu: Tom Lea Paints Island Invasion." *Life* v18n24 (June 11, 1945): 61-67.

Leckie, Robert. *Helmet for My Pillow*. New York: Doubleday, 1979,

Leckie, Robert. *Strong Men Armed*. New York: DaCapo Press, 1997.

McMillan, George. *Old Breed: A History of the First Marine Division in World War II*. Washington, DC: Infantry Journal Press, 1949.

Moran, Jim. *Peleliu 1944: The Forgotten Corner of Hell*. Westport, CT: Praeger Publishing, 2004.

O'Dell, James Douglas. *The Water is Never Cold: The Origins of U.S. Naval Combat Demolition Units, UDTs, and Seals.* Dulles, Virginia: Brasseys, Inc., 2000.

O'Donnell, Patrick. *Into the Rising Sun: In Their Own Words, World War II's Pacific Veterans Reveal the Heart of Combat.* New York: Free Press, 2002.

Pope, Everett. Telephone interview. 4 August 2002.

Raynor, Bill. E-mail to author. 28 March 2004.

Ross, Bill. *Peleliu: Tragic Triumph.* New York: Random House, 1991.

Sherrod, Robert. *History of Marine Corps Aviation in World War II.* Baltimore, Maryland : The Nautical & Aviation Publishing Company of America, 1987.

Sledge, Eugene. *With the Old Breed: At Peleliu and Okinawa.* Novato California: Presidio Press, 1981.

Smith, Robert Ross. *The Approach to the Philippines.* Washington : Office of the Chief of Military History, Dept. of the Army, 1953.

Stewart, William H. *Ghost Fleet of the Truk Lagoon.* Missoula, Montana: Pictorial Histories Publishing Company, 1985.

Wagner, Corydon. "The Bones of Nakagawa." *Naval History.* Washington, D.C.: United States Naval Institute, February 2003.

Wees, Paul Marshall, M.D. *King-Doctor of Ulithi.* New York: The Macmillan Company, 1950.

Wheeler, Richard. *A Special Valor, The Marines and the Pacific War.* New York: Harper & Row, 1983.

Wheeler, Richard. *Iwo.* New York: Lippincott & Crowell, Publishers, 1983.

Young, Darryl. *Seals, UDT, Frogmen: Men Under Pressure.* Toronto: Ballantine Books, 1994.

Index

188

About the Author

Patrick M. Finelli is a writer, historian, scuba diving enthusiast and professor at the University of South Florida. He was born in Boston and educated at the University of California at Berkeley where he earned the B.A., M.A. and Ph.D. degrees. He also holds an M.B.A. He has written over 300 articles on historical topics and technology since 1982. His first book was published in 1989. He is the founder of Pfweb.com, the host of the tribute website for Peleliu and his father's 1st Marine Division service in World War II: The URL is: http://www.pfweb.com/plf-usmc/